THIS BELONGS TO

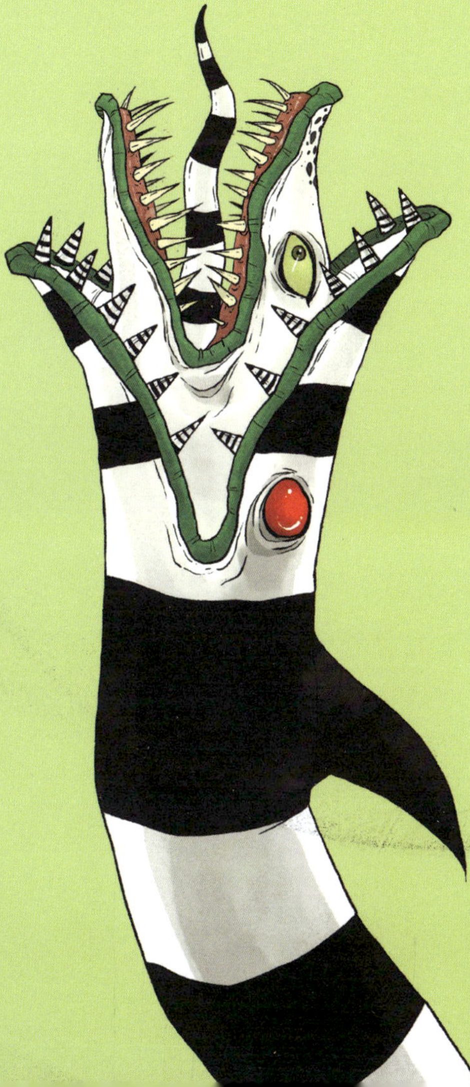

DATE __/__/__

TAROT READING

MOON PHASE

Who is the tarot spread for?

QUERY

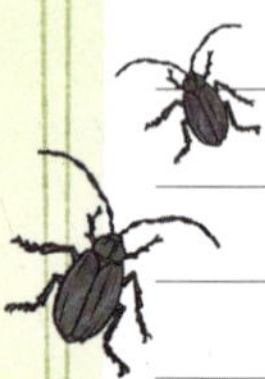

CARDS SELECTED

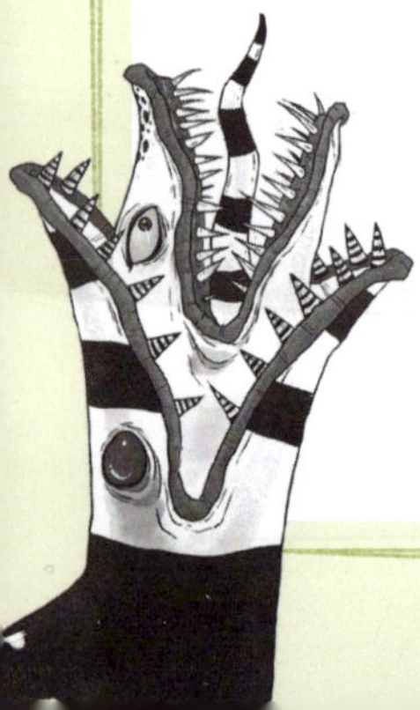

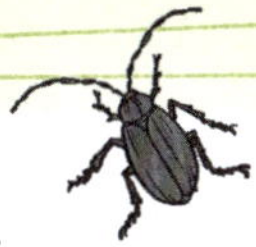

TAROT READING

INTERPRETATIONS

Thoughts and feelings:

DRAW YOUR SPREADS HERE

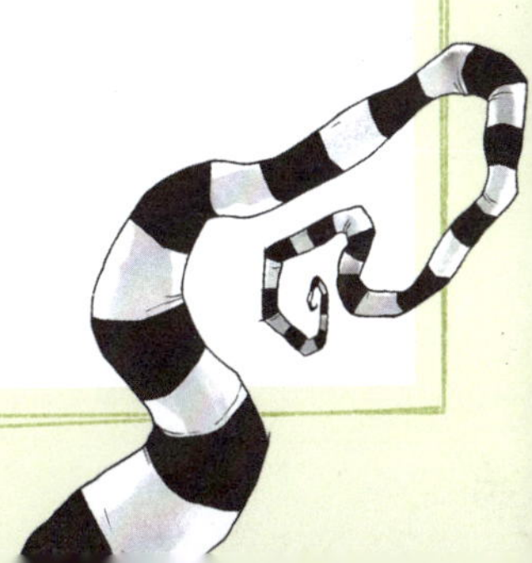

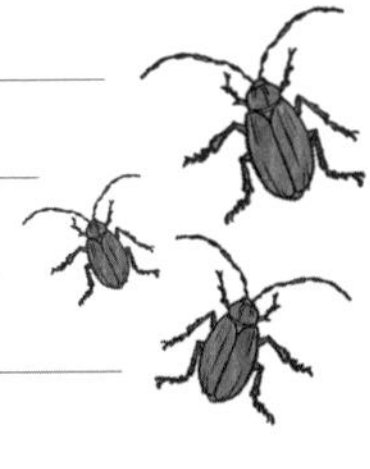

DATE __/__/__

TAROT READING

MOON PHASE

Who is the tarot spread for?

QUERY

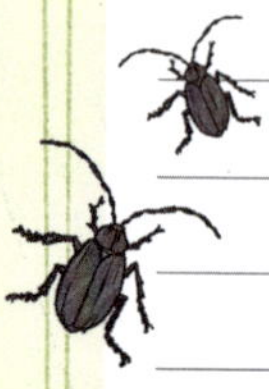

CARDS SELECTED

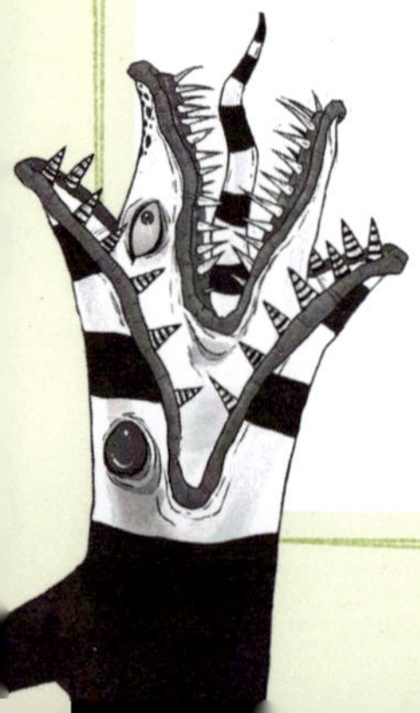

TAROT READING

INTERPRETATIONS

Thoughts and feelings:

DRAW YOUR SPREADS HERE

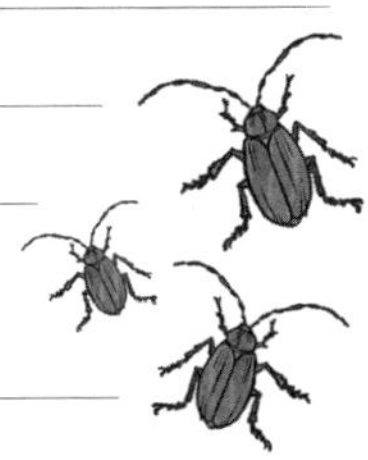

DATE __/__/__

TAROT READING

MOON PHASE

Who is the tarot spread for?

QUERY

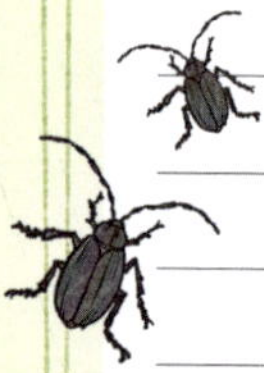

CARDS SELECTED

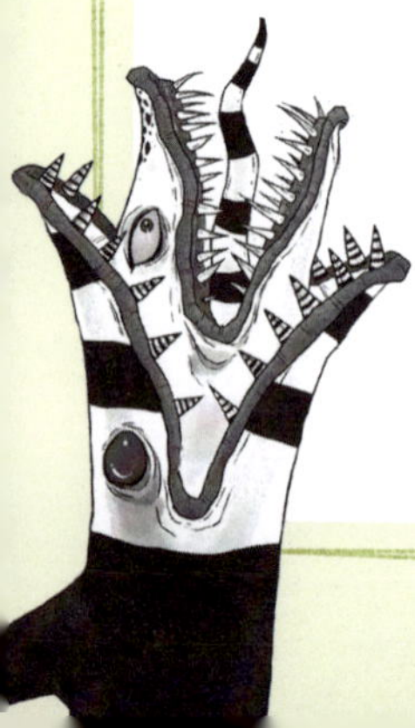

TAROT READING

INTERPRETATIONS

Thoughts and feelings:

DRAW YOUR SPREADS HERE

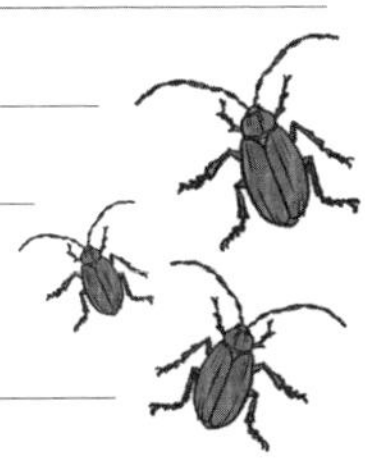

DATE __/__/__

TAROT READING

MOON PHASE

Who is the tarot spread for?

QUERY

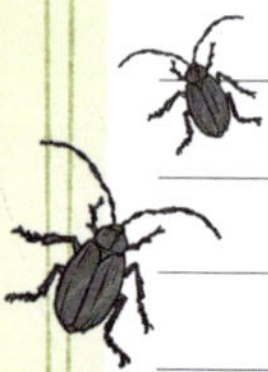

CARDS SELECTED

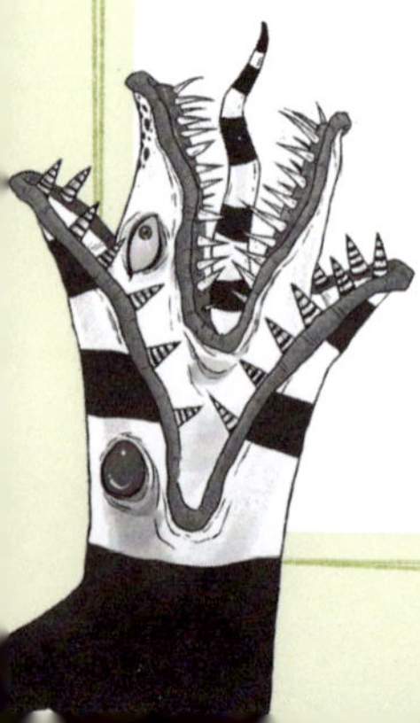

TAROT READING

INTERPRETATIONS

Thoughts and feelings:

DRAW YOUR SPREADS HERE

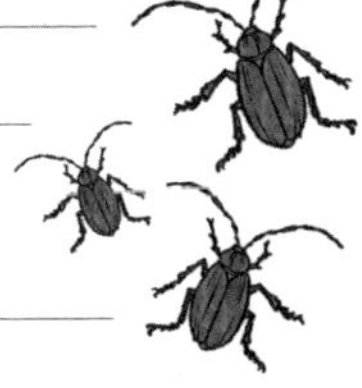

DATE __/__/__

TAROT READING

MOON PHASE

Who is the tarot spread for?

QUERY

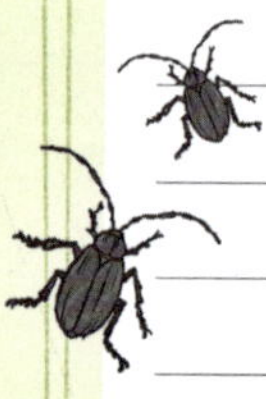

CARDS SELECTED

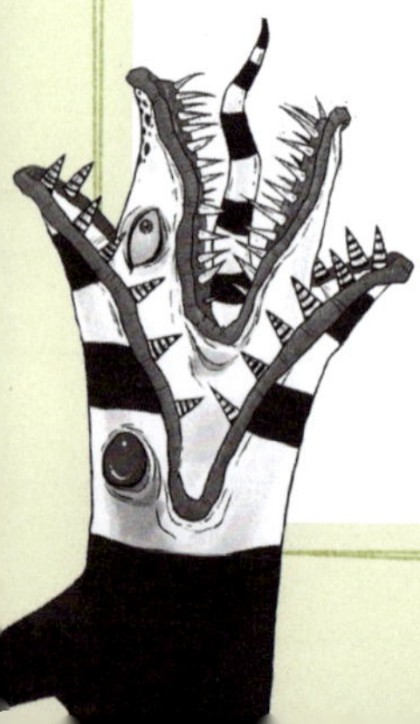

TAROT READING

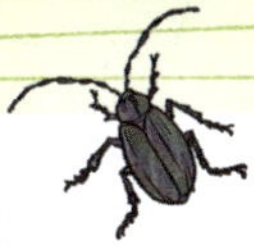

INTERPRETATIONS

Thoughts and feelings:

DRAW YOUR SPREADS HERE

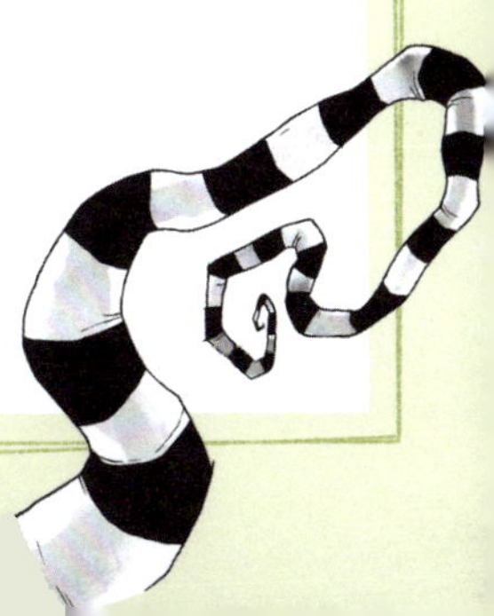

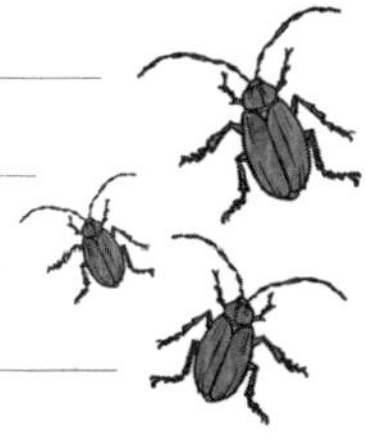

DATE __/__/__

TAROT READING

MOON PHASE

Who is the tarot spread for?

QUERY

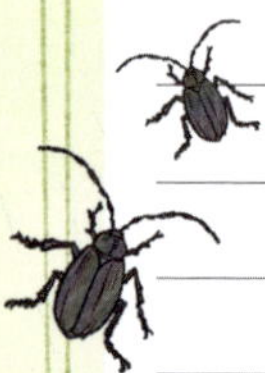

CARDS SELECTED

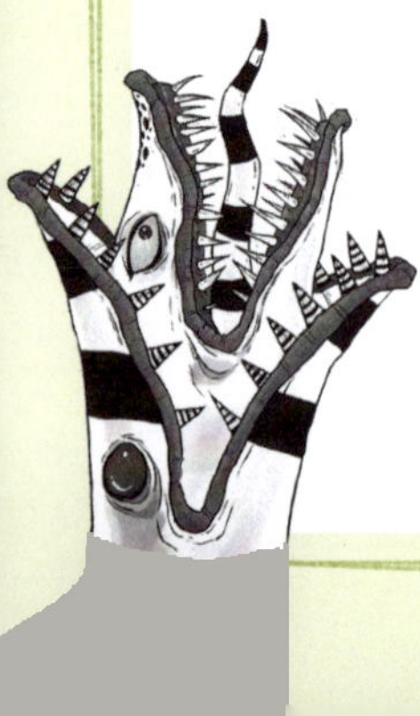

TAROT READING

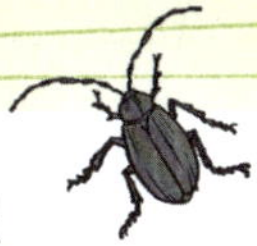

INTERPRETATIONS

Thoughts and feelings:

DRAW YOUR SPREADS HERE

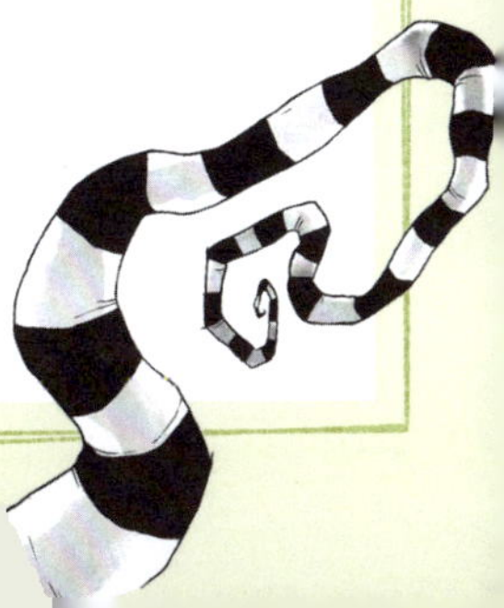

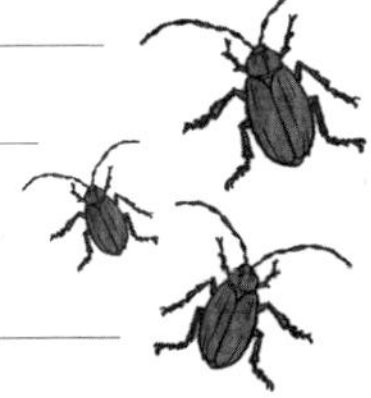

DATE __/__/__

TAROT READING

MOON PHASE

Who is the tarot spread for?

QUERY

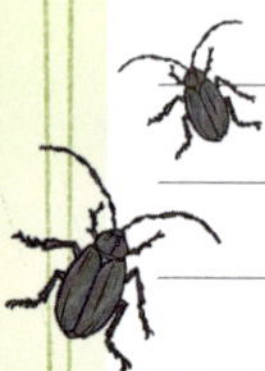

CARDS SELECTED

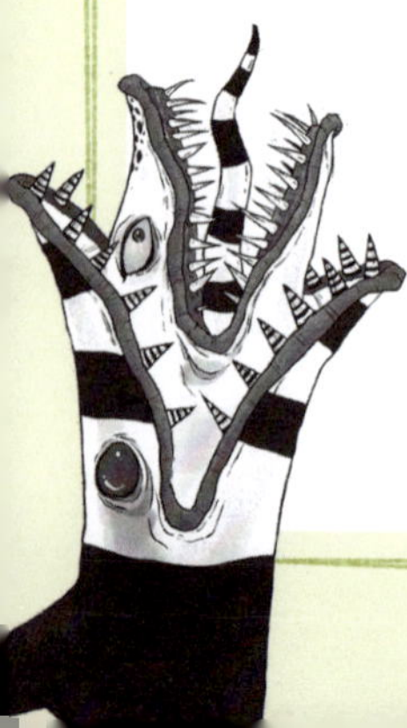

TAROT READING

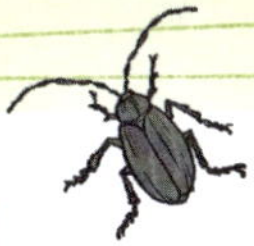

INTERPRETATIONS

Thoughts and feelings:

DRAW YOUR SPREADS HERE

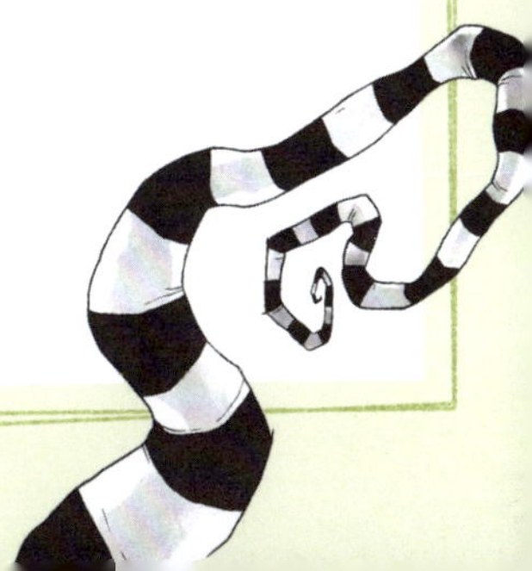

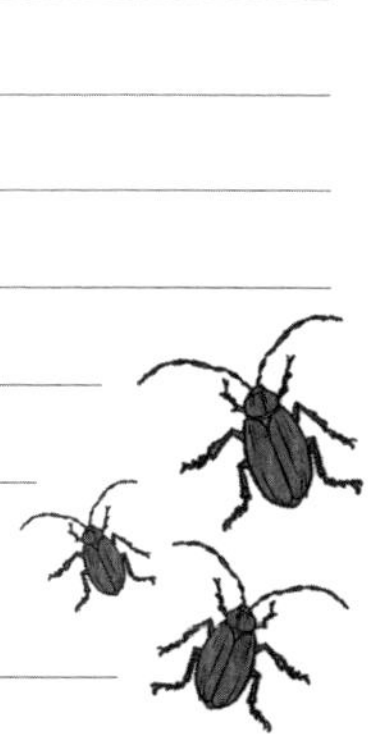

DATE __/__/__

TAROT READING

MOON PHASE

Who is the tarot spread for?

QUERY

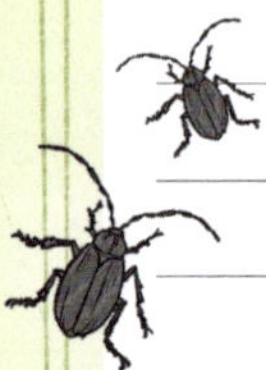

CARDS SELECTED

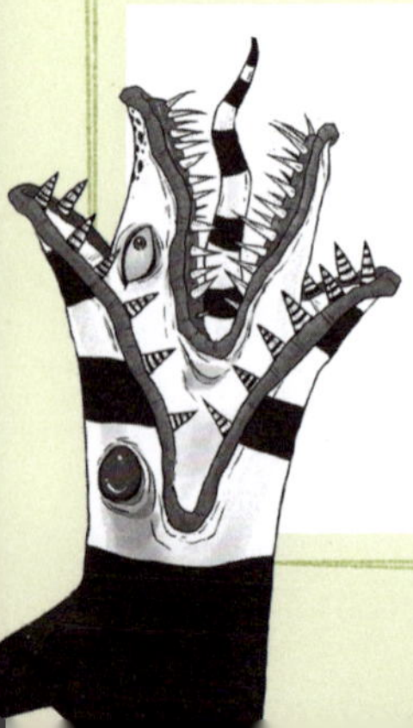

TAROT READING

INTERPRETATIONS

Thoughts and feelings:

DRAW YOUR SPREADS HERE

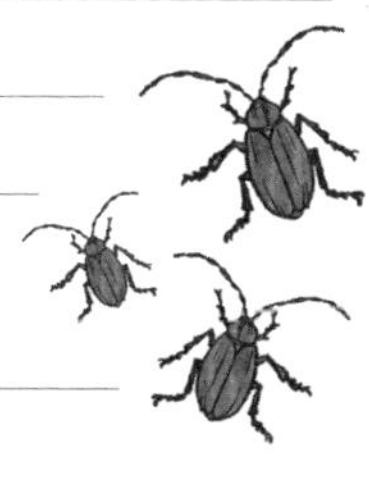

DATE __/__/__

TAROT READING

MOON PHASE

Who is the tarot spread for?

QUERY

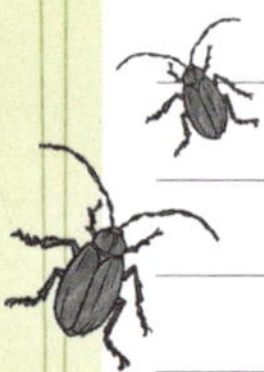

CARDS SELECTED

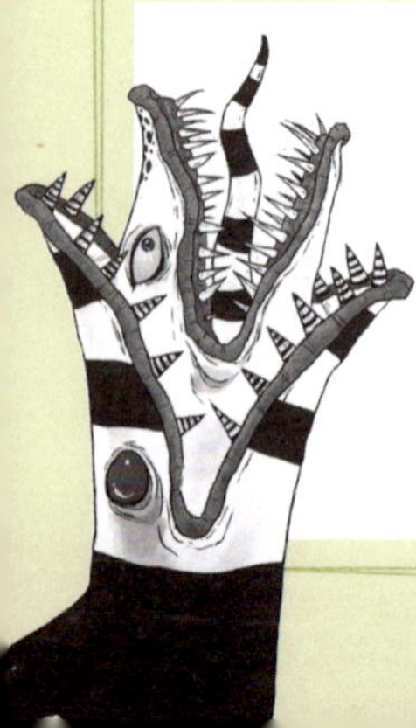

TAROT READING

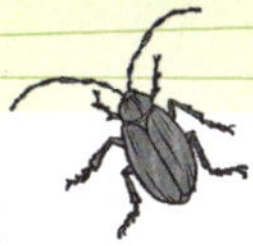

INTERPRETATIONS

Thoughts and feelings:

DRAW YOUR SPREADS HERE

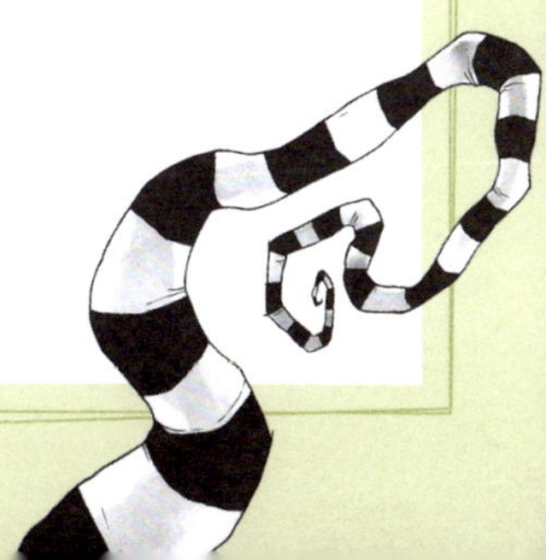

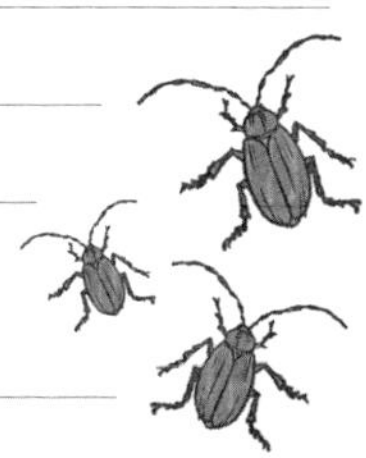

DATE __/__/__

TAROT READING

MOON PHASE

Who is the tarot spread for?

QUERY

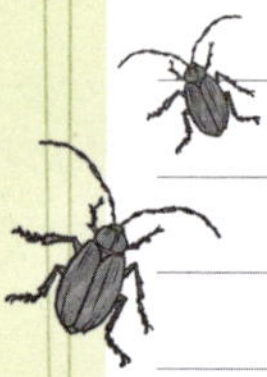

CARDS SELECTED

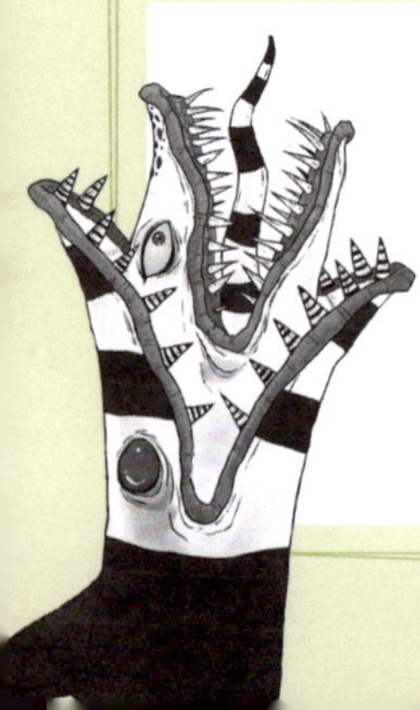

TAROT READING

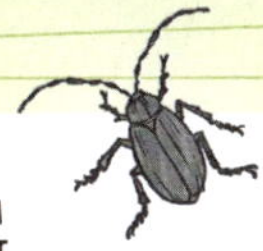

INTERPRETATIONS

Thoughts and feelings:

DRAW YOUR SPREADS HERE

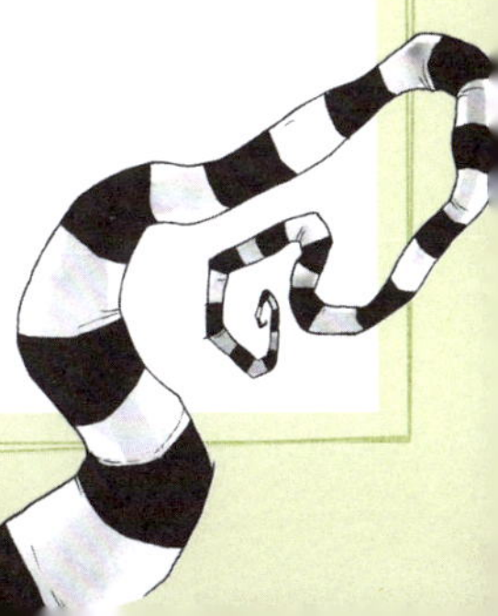

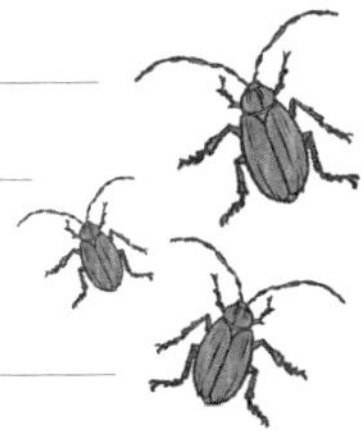

DATE __/__/__

TAROT READING

MOON PHASE

Who is the tarot spread for?

QUERY

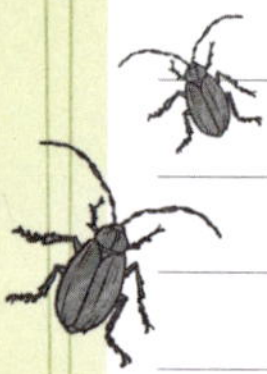

CARDS SELECTED

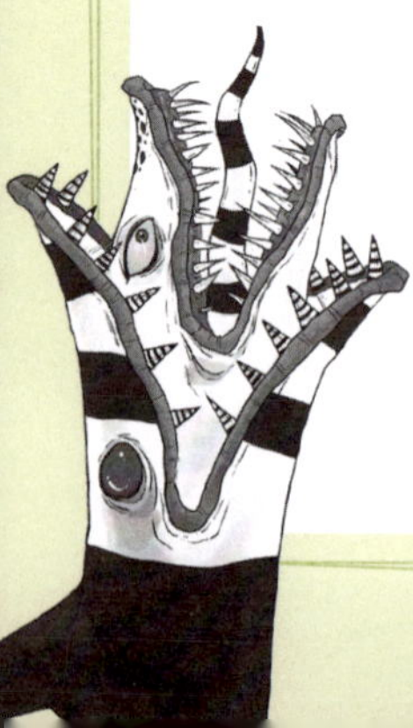

TAROT READING

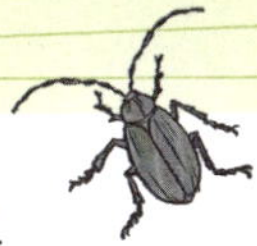

INTERPRETATIONS

Thoughts and feelings:

DRAW YOUR SPREADS HERE

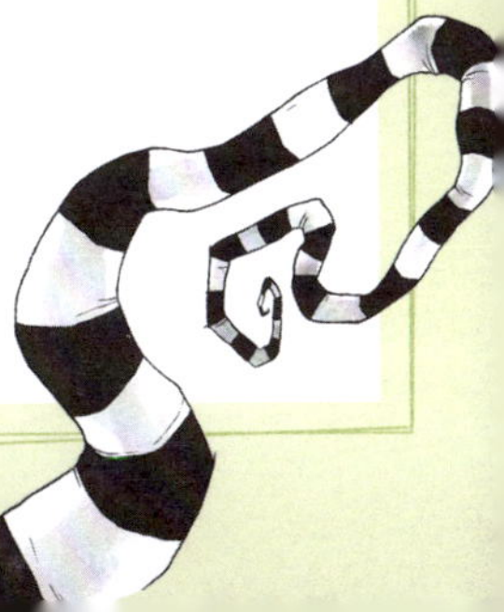

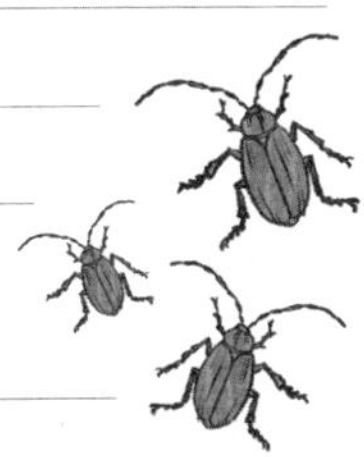

DATE __/__/__

TAROT READING

MOON PHASE

Who is the tarot spread for?

QUERY

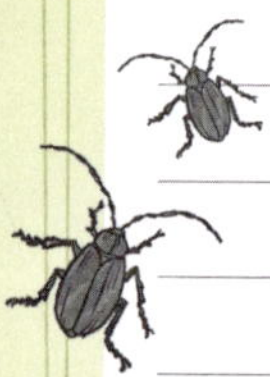

CARDS SELECTED

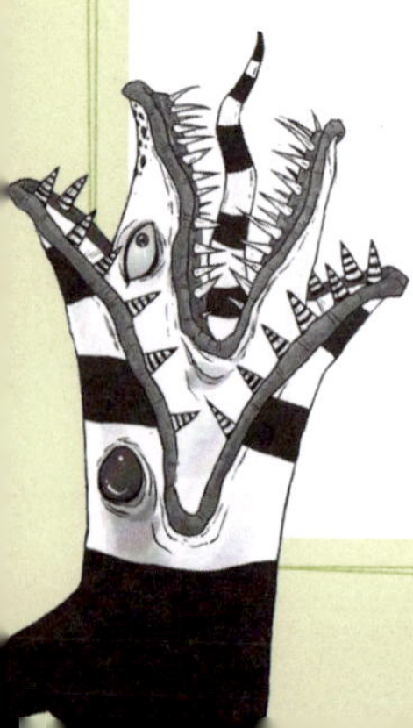

TAROT READING

INTERPRETATIONS

Thoughts and feelings:

DRAW YOUR SPREADS HERE

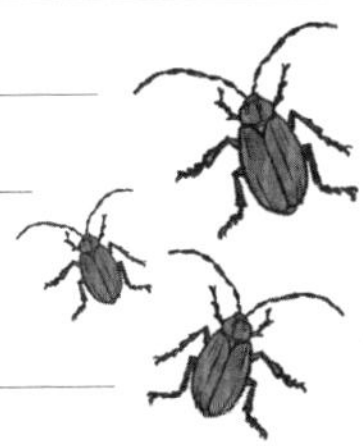

DATE __/__/__

TAROT READING

MOON PHASE

Who is the tarot spread for?

QUERY

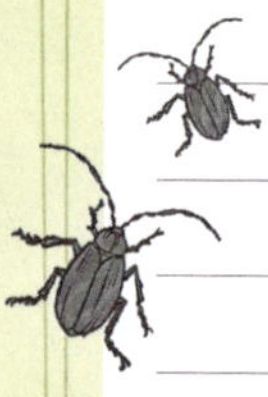

CARDS SELECTED

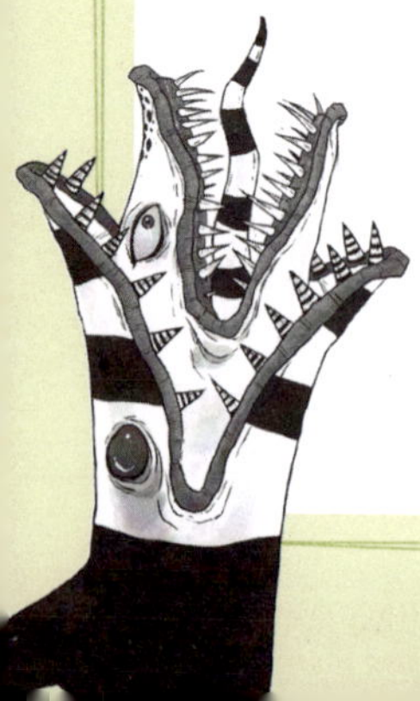

TAROT READING

INTERPRETATIONS

Thoughts and feelings:

DRAW YOUR SPREADS HERE

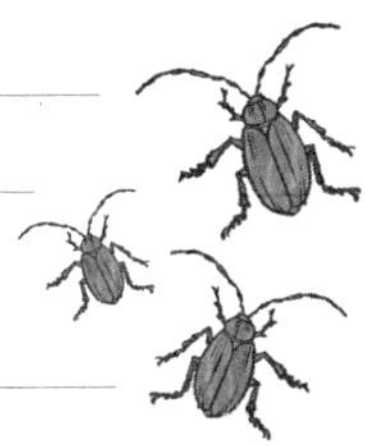

DATE __/__/__

TAROT READING

MOON PHASE

Who is the tarot spread for?

QUERY

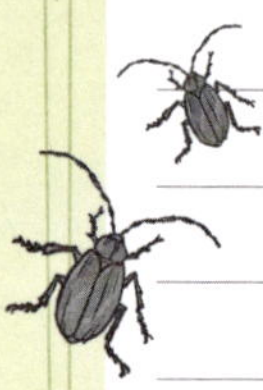

CARDS SELECTED

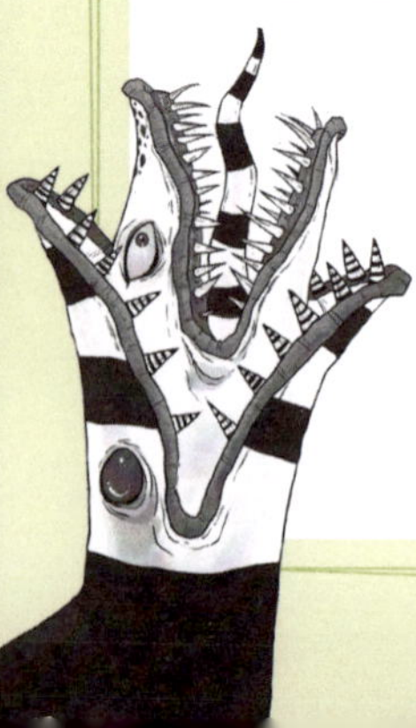

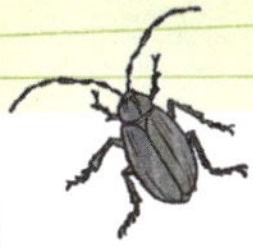

TAROT READING

INTERPRETATIONS

Thoughts and feelings:

DRAW YOUR SPREADS HERE

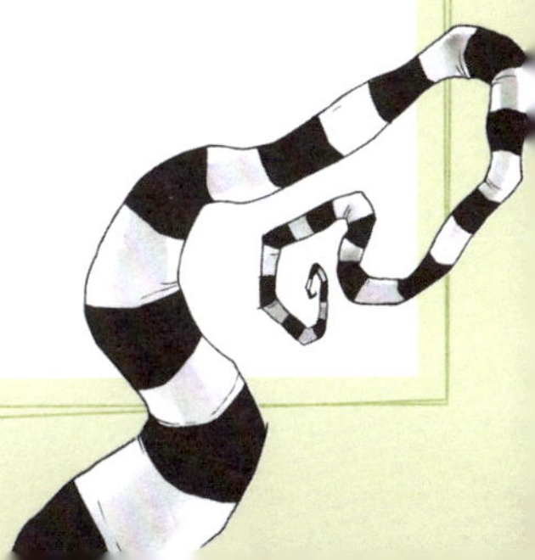

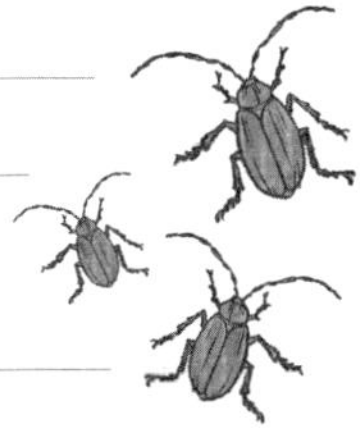

DATE __/__/__

TAROT READING

MOON PHASE

Who is the tarot spread for?

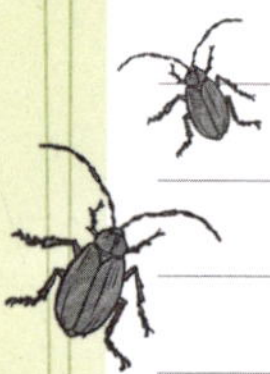

QUERY

CARDS SELECTED

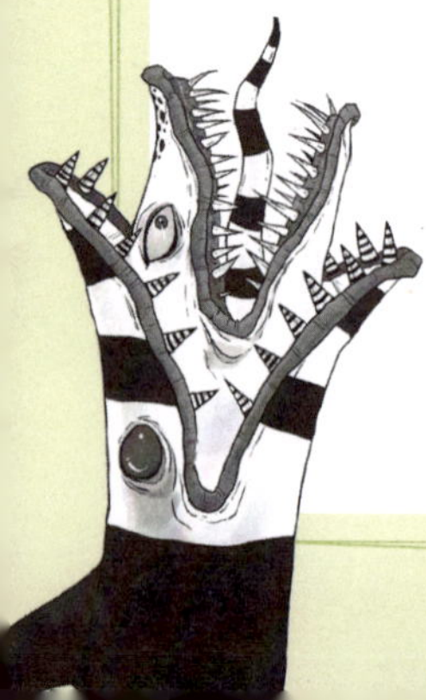

TAROT READING

INTERPRETATIONS

Thoughts and feelings:

DRAW YOUR SPREADS HERE

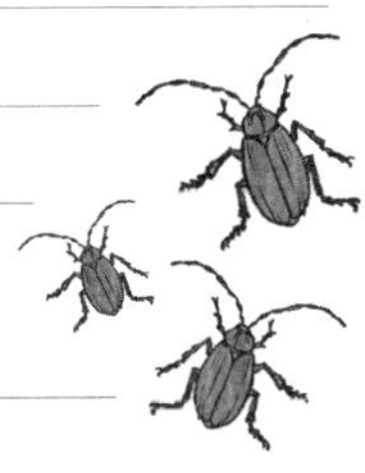

DATE __/__/__

TAROT READING

MOON PHASE

Who is the tarot spread for?

QUERY

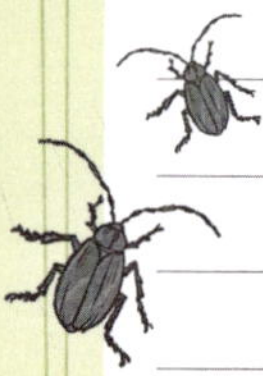

CARDS SELECTED

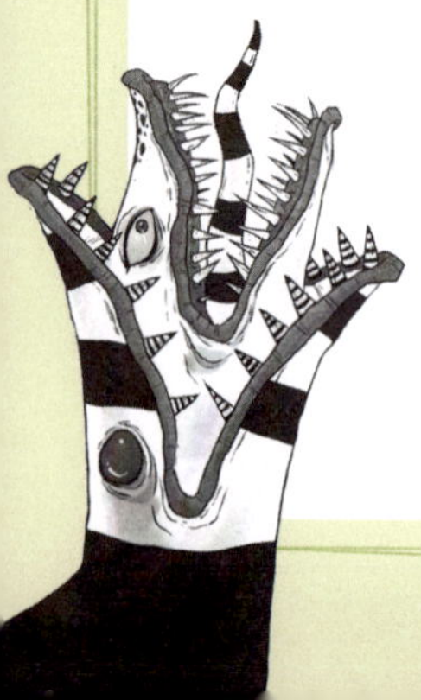

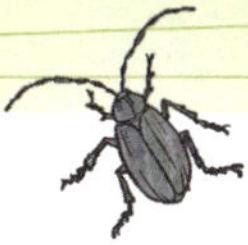

TAROT READING

INTERPRETATIONS

Thoughts and feelings:

DRAW YOUR SPREADS HERE

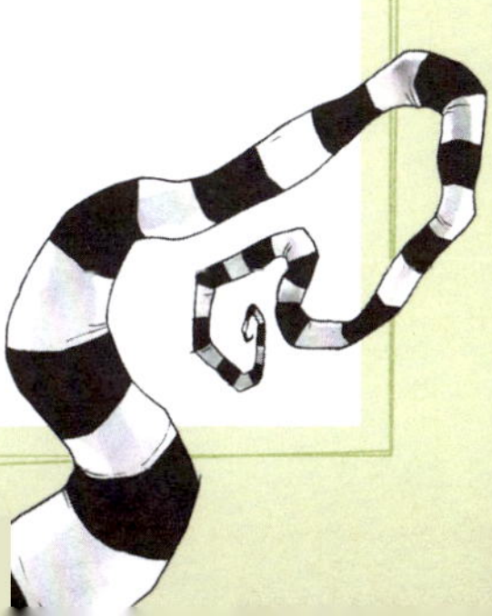

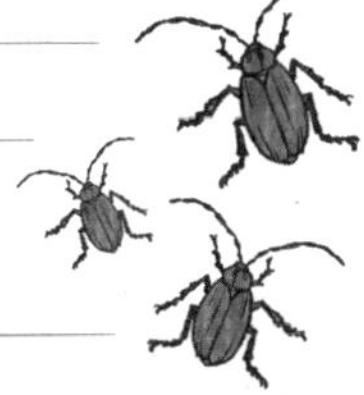

DATE __/__/__

TAROT READING

MOON PHASE

Who is the tarot spread for?

QUERY

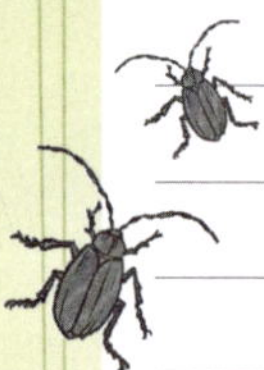

CARDS SELECTED

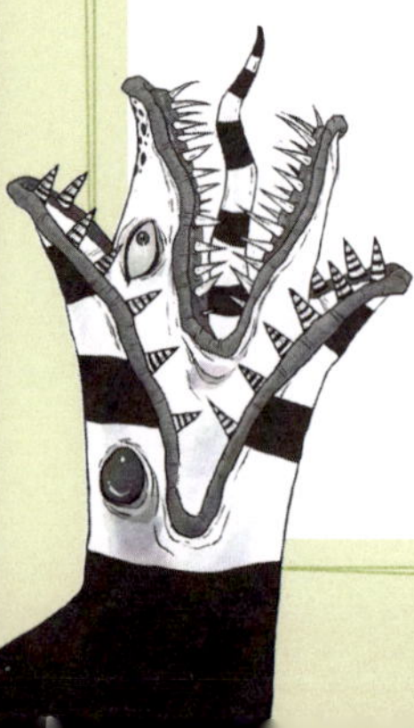

TAROT READING

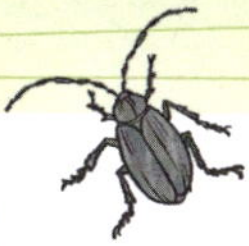

INTERPRETATIONS

Thoughts and feelings:

DRAW YOUR SPREADS HERE

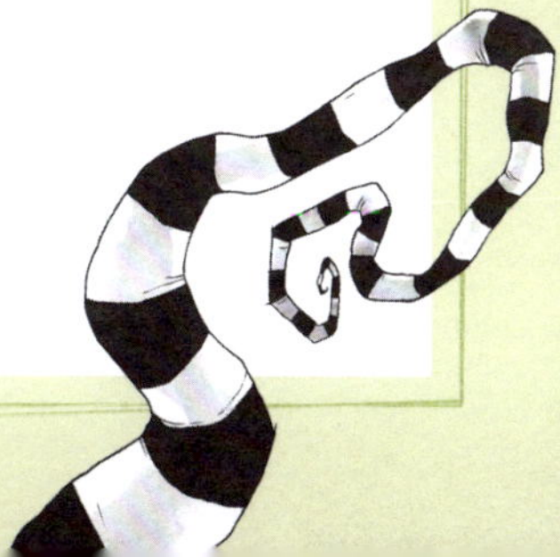

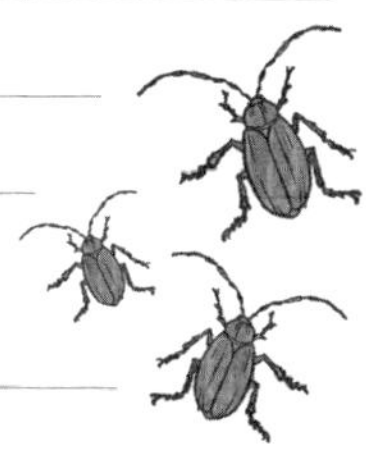

DATE __/__/__

TAROT READING

MOON PHASE

Who is the tarot spread for?

QUERY

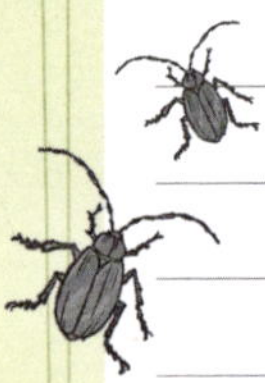

CARDS SELECTED

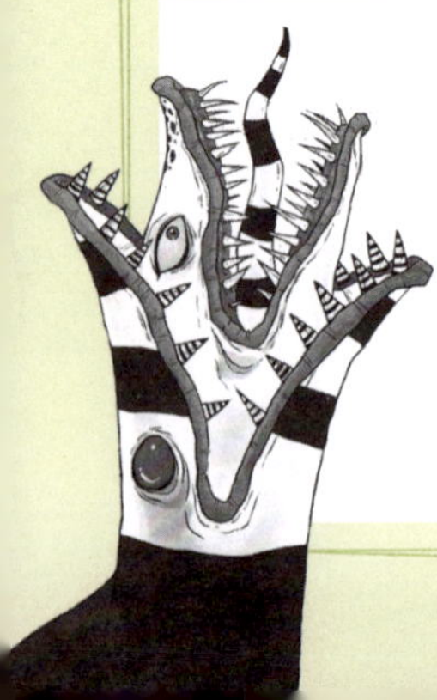

TAROT READING

INTERPRETATIONS

Thoughts and feelings:

DRAW YOUR SPREADS HERE

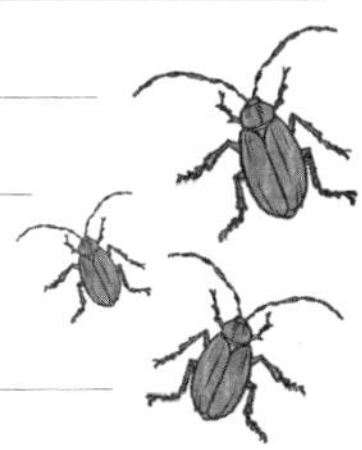

DATE __/__/__

TAROT READING

MOON PHASE

Who is the tarot spread for?

QUERY

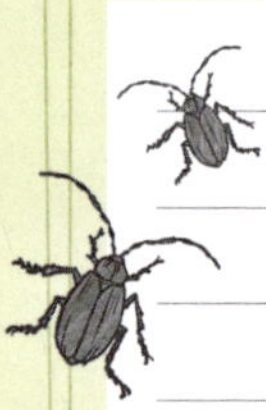

CARDS SELECTED

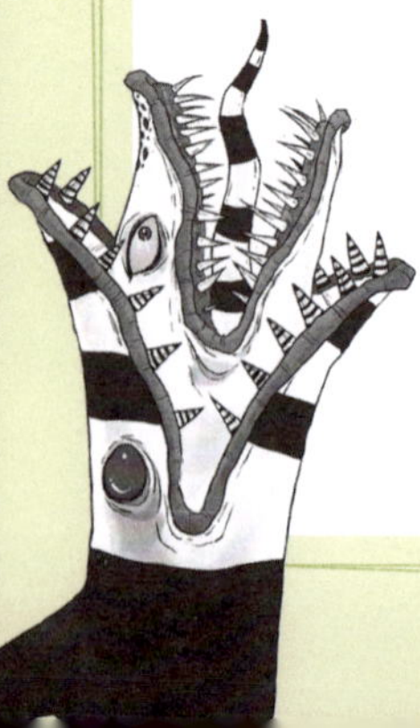

TAROT READING

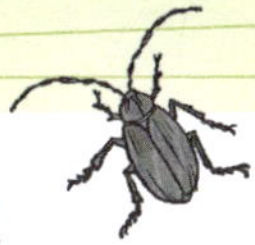

INTERPRETATIONS

Thoughts and feelings:

DRAW YOUR SPREADS HERE

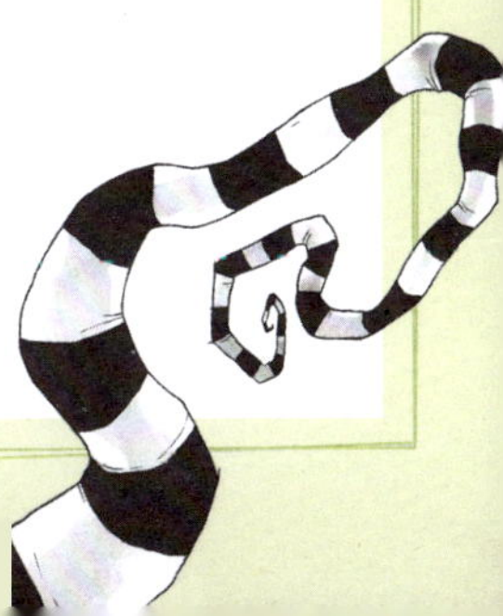

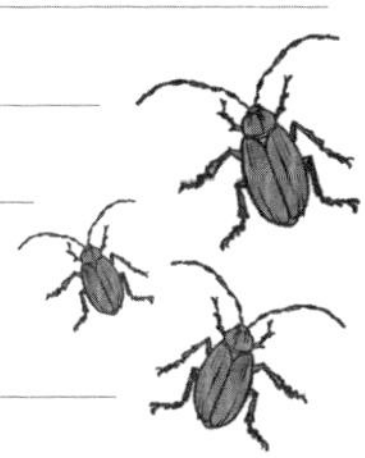

DATE __/__/__

TAROT READING

MOON PHASE

Who is the tarot spread for?

QUERY

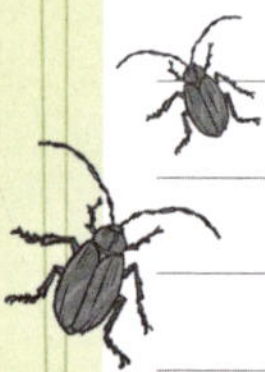

CARDS SELECTED

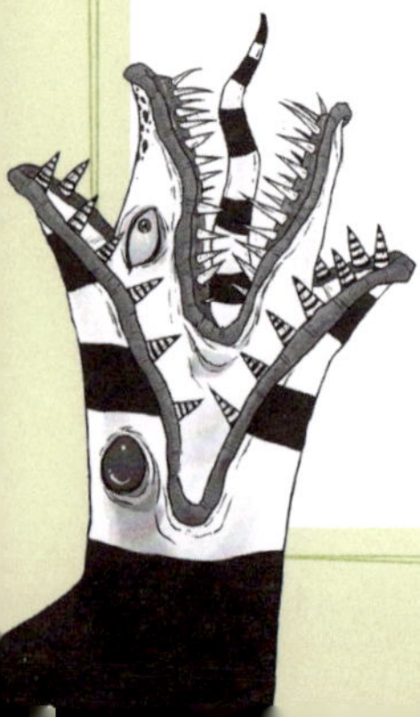

TAROT READING

INTERPRETATIONS

Thoughts and feelings:

DRAW YOUR SPREADS HERE

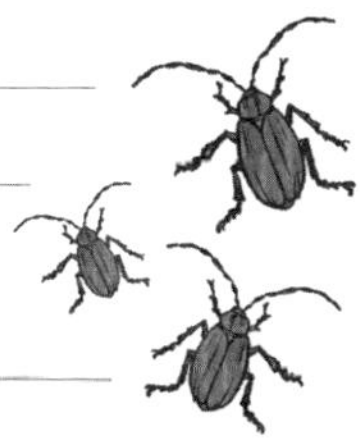

DATE __/__/__

TAROT READING

MOON PHASE

Who is the tarot spread for?

QUERY

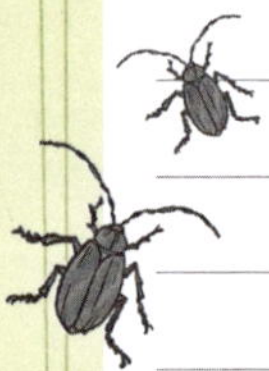

CARDS SELECTED

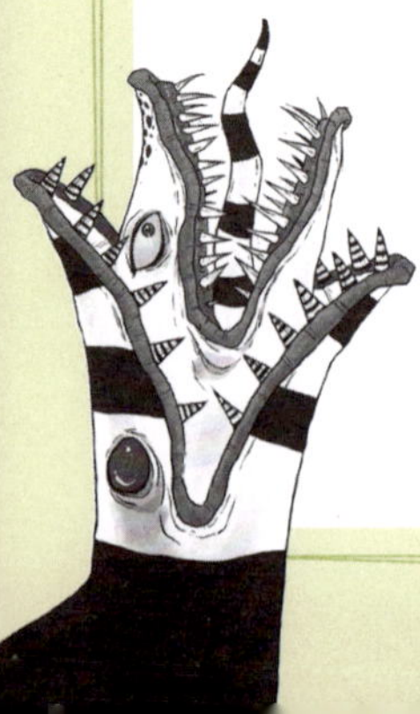

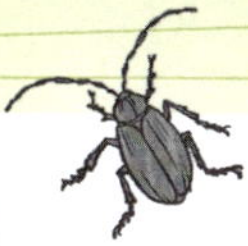

Tarot Reading

INTERPRETATIONS

Thoughts and feelings:

DRAW YOUR SPREADS HERE

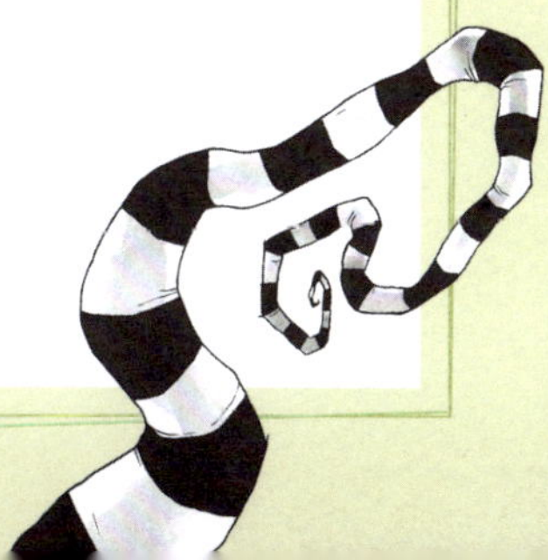

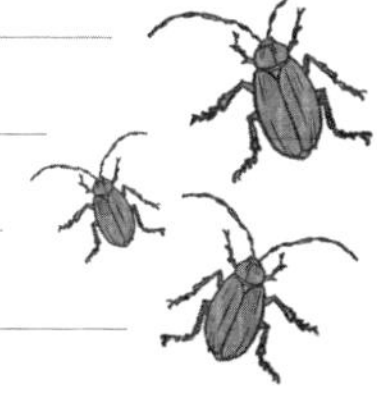

DATE __/__/__

TAROT READING

MOON PHASE

Who is the tarot spread for?

QUERY

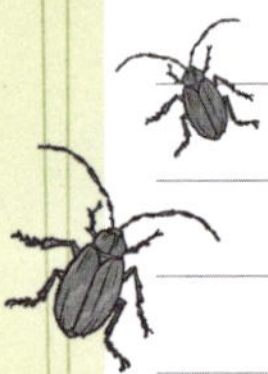

CARDS SELECTED

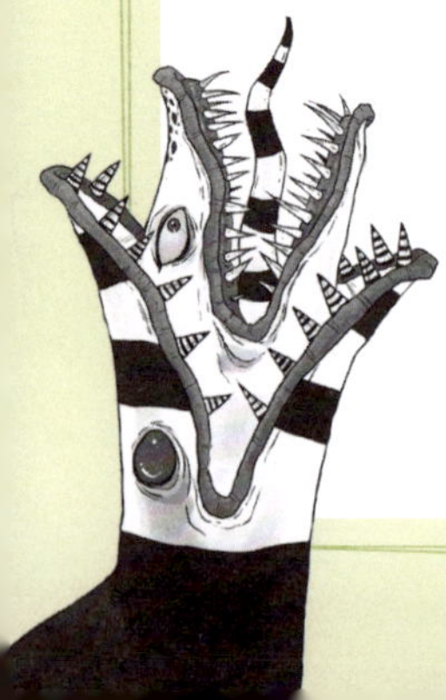

TAROT READING

INTERPRETATIONS

Thoughts and feelings:

DRAW YOUR SPREADS HERE

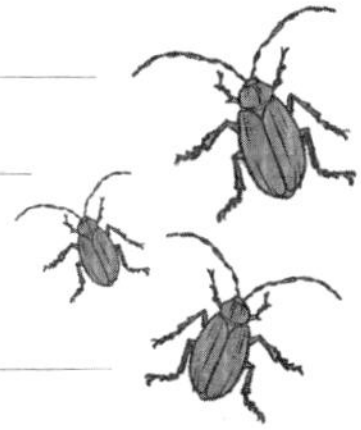

DATE __/__/__

TAROT READING

MOON PHASE

Who is the tarot spread for?

QUERY

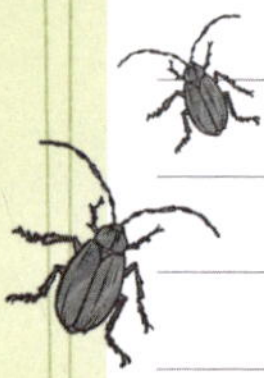

CARDS SELECTED

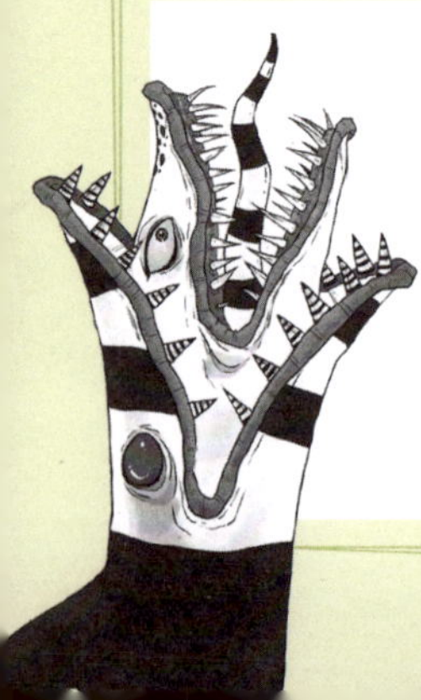

TAROT READING

INTERPRETATIONS

Thoughts and feelings:

DRAW YOUR SPREADS HERE

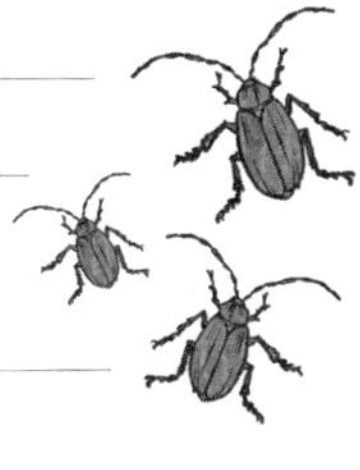

DATE __/__/__

TAROT READING

MOON PHASE

Who is the tarot spread for?

QUERY

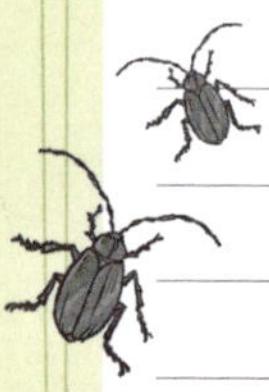

CARDS SELECTED

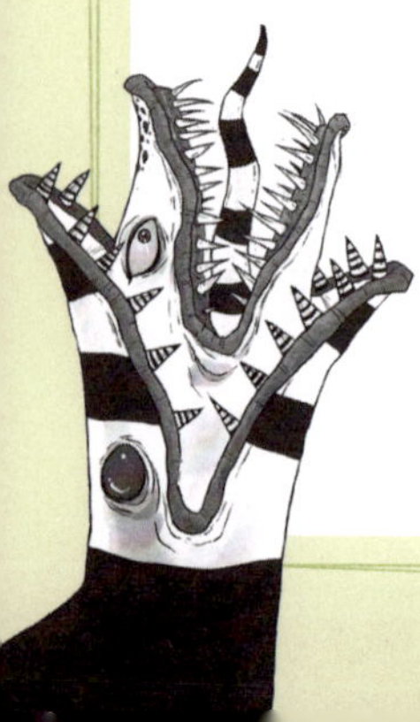

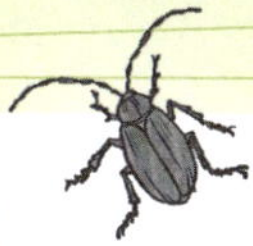

TAROT READING

INTERPRETATIONS

Thoughts and feelings:

DRAW YOUR SPREADS HERE

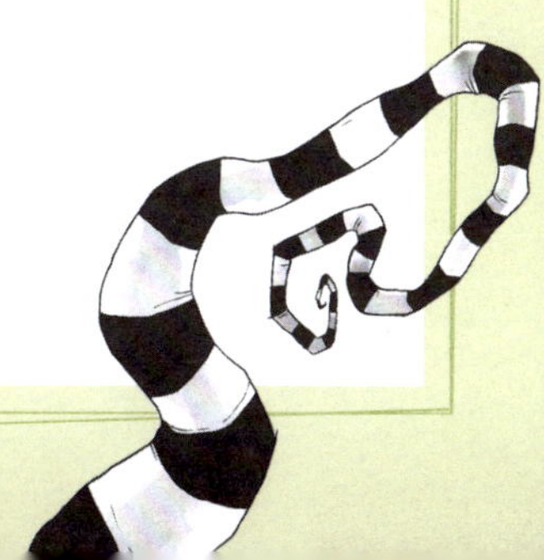

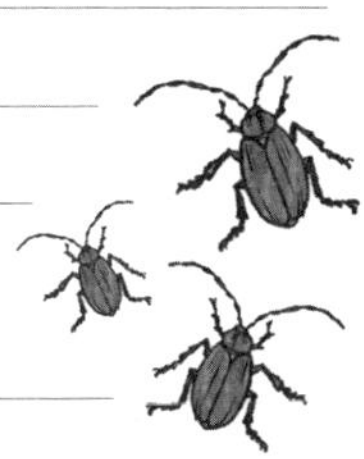

DATE __/__/__

TAROT READING

MOON PHASE

Who is the tarot spread for?

QUERY

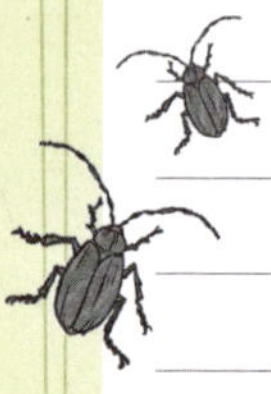

CARDS SELECTED

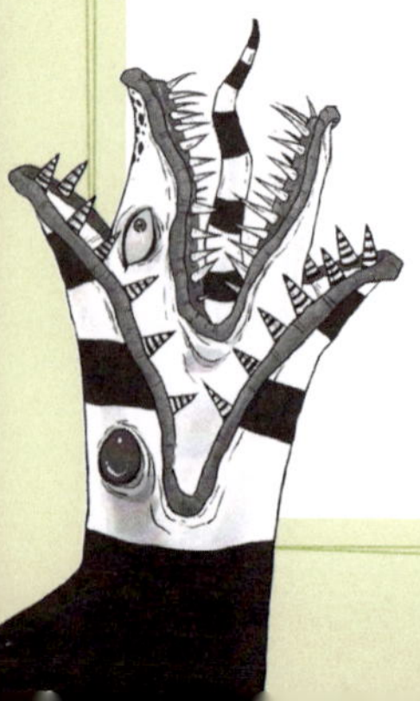

TAROT READING

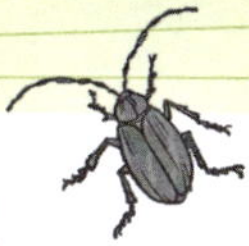

INTERPRETATIONS

Thoughts and feelings:

DRAW YOUR SPREADS HERE

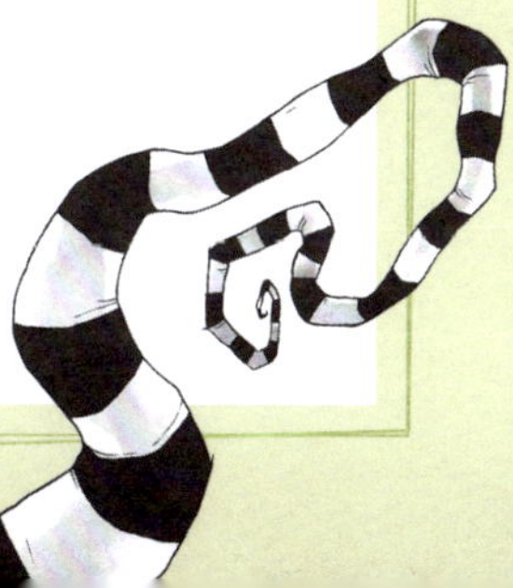

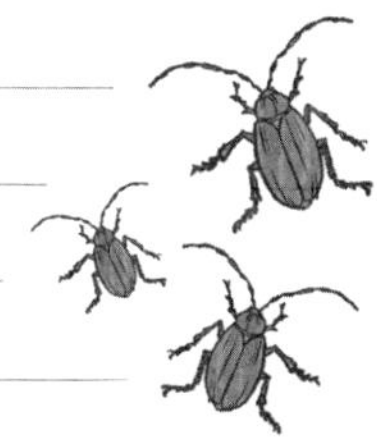

DATE __/__/__

TAROT READING

MOON PHASE

Who is the tarot spread for?

QUERY

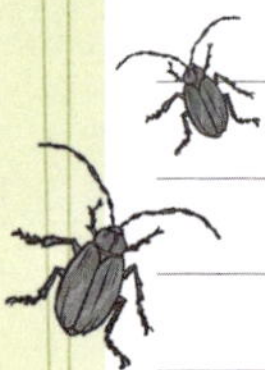

CARDS SELECTED

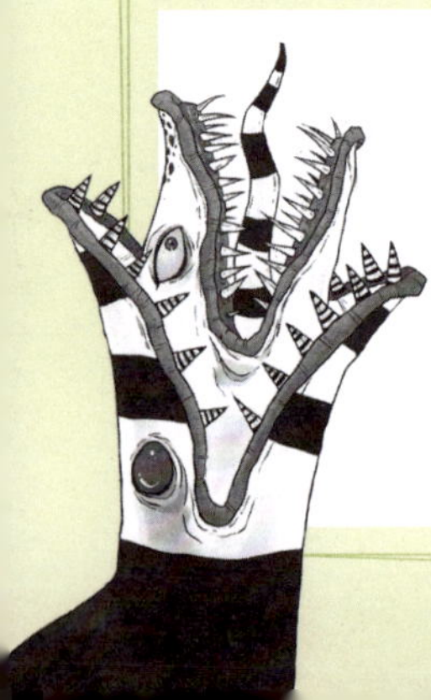

Tarot Reading

INTERPRETATIONS

Thoughts and feelings:

DRAW YOUR SPREADS HERE

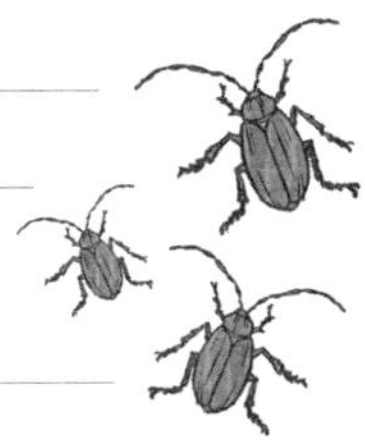

DATE __/__/__

TAROT READING

MOON PHASE

Who is the tarot spread for?

QUERY

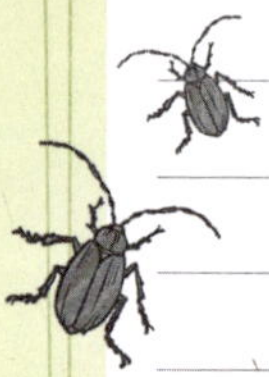

CARDS SELECTED

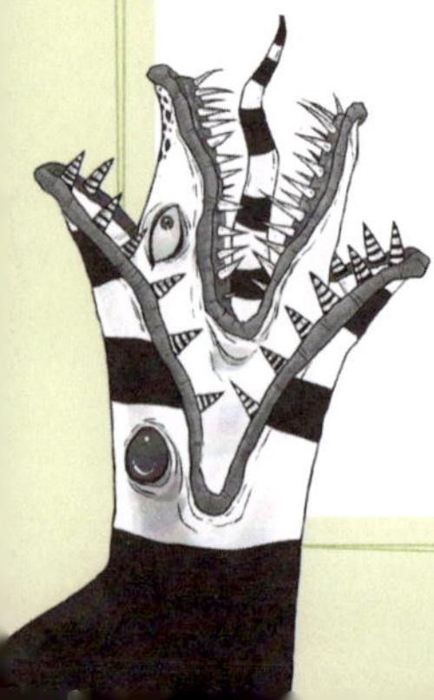

TAROT READING

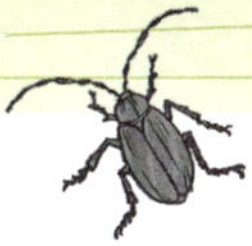

INTERPRETATIONS

Thoughts and feelings:

DRAW YOUR SPREADS HERE

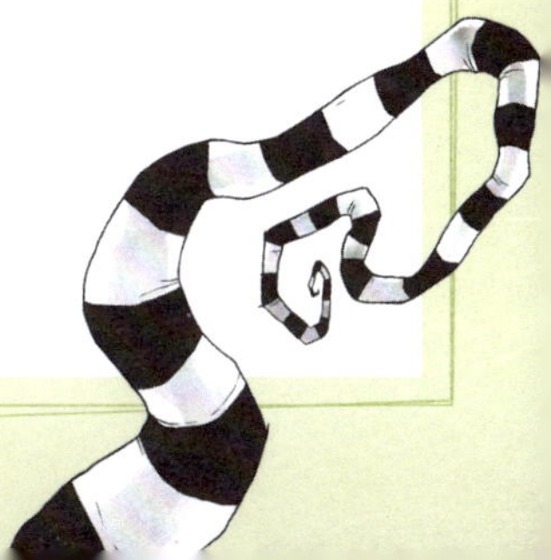

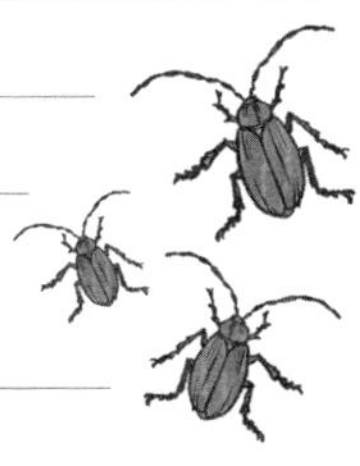

DATE __/__/__

TAROT READING

MOON PHASE

Who is the tarot spread for?

QUERY

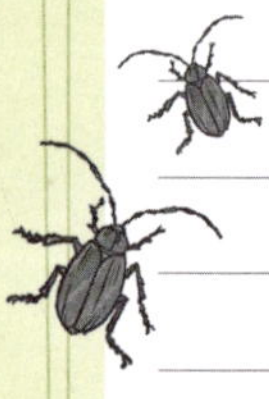

CARDS SELECTED

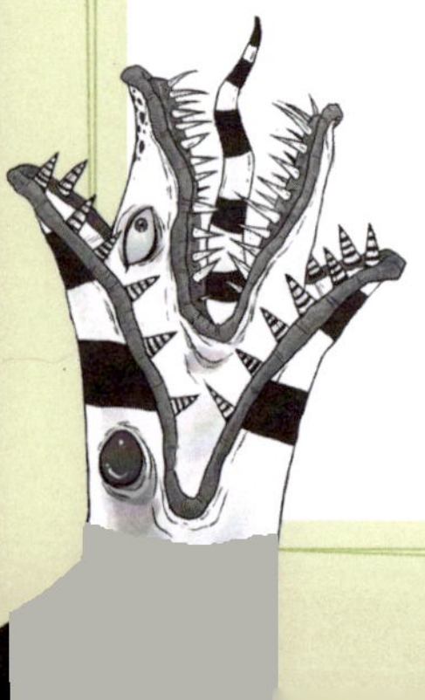

TAROT READING

INTERPRETATIONS

Thoughts and feelings:

DRAW YOUR SPREADS HERE

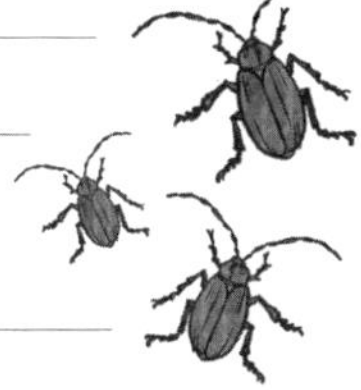

DATE __/__/__

TAROT READING

MOON PHASE

Who is the tarot spread for?

QUERY

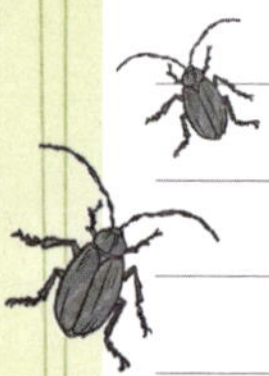

CARDS SELECTED

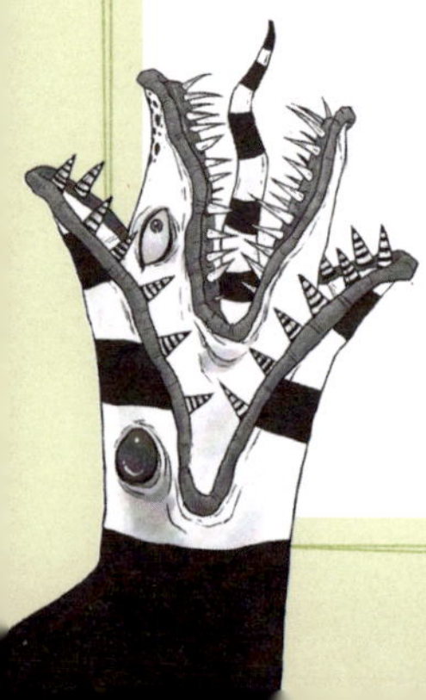

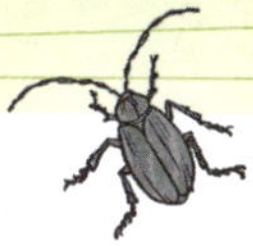

Tarot Reading

INTERPRETATIONS

Thoughts and feelings:

DRAW YOUR SPREADS HERE

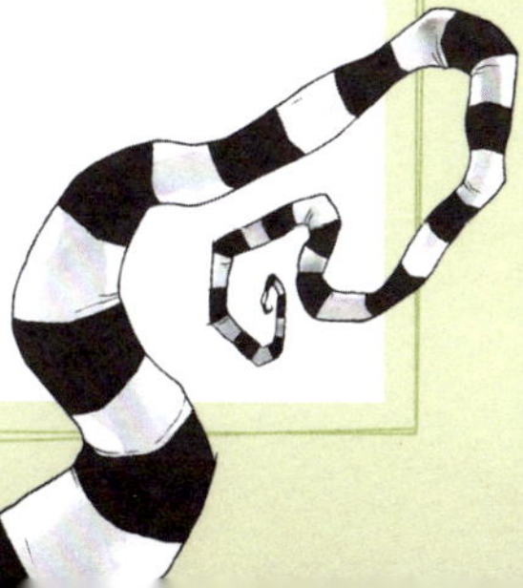

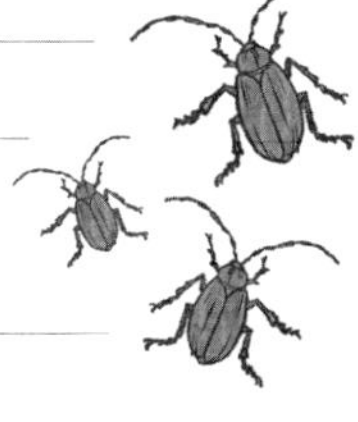

DATE __/__/__

TAROT READING

MOON PHASE

Who is the tarot spread for?

QUERY

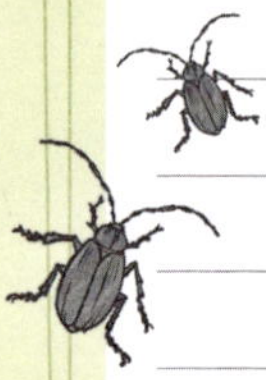

CARDS SELECTED

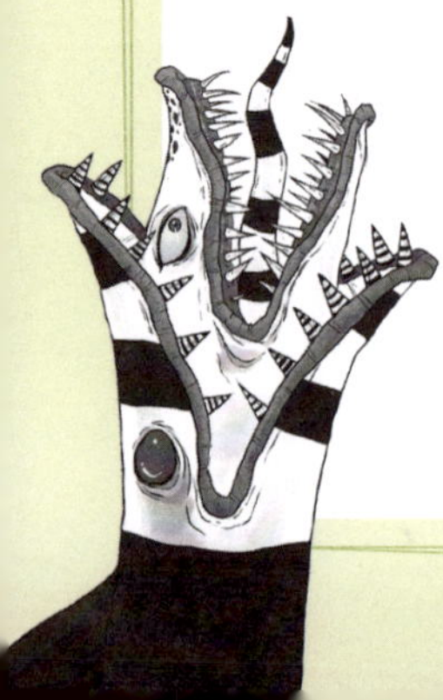

TAROT READING

INTERPRETATIONS

Thoughts and feelings:

DRAW YOUR SPREADS HERE

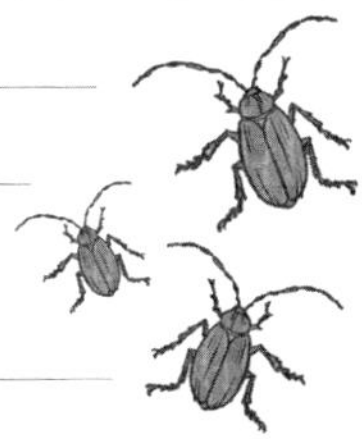

DATE __/__/__

TAROT READING

MOON PHASE

Who is the tarot spread for?

QUERY

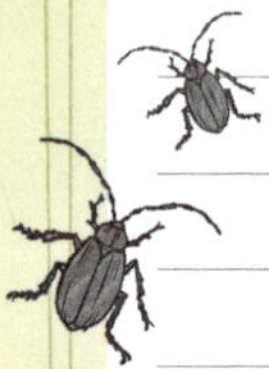

CARDS SELECTED

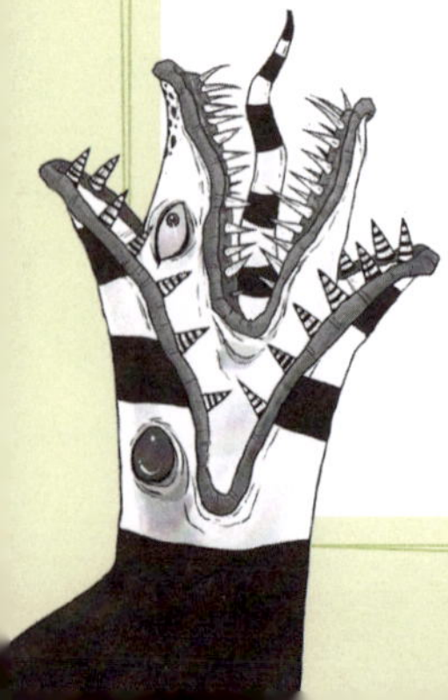

TAROT READING

INTERPRETATIONS

Thoughts and feelings:

DRAW YOUR SPREADS HERE

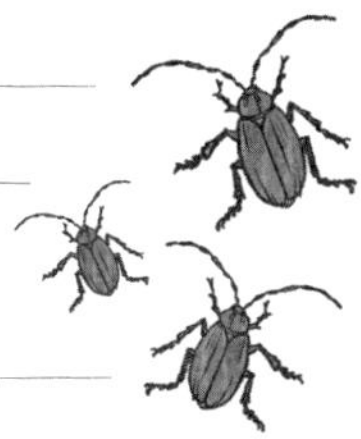

DATE __/__/__

TAROT READING

MOON PHASE

Who is the tarot spread for?

QUERY

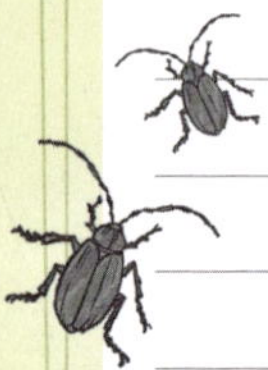

CARDS SELECTED

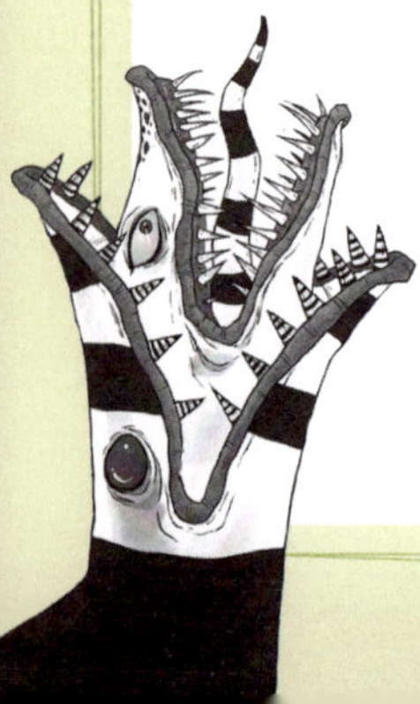

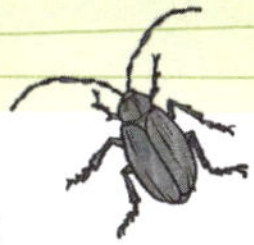

TAROT READING

INTERPRETATIONS

Thoughts and feelings:

DRAW YOUR SPREADS HERE

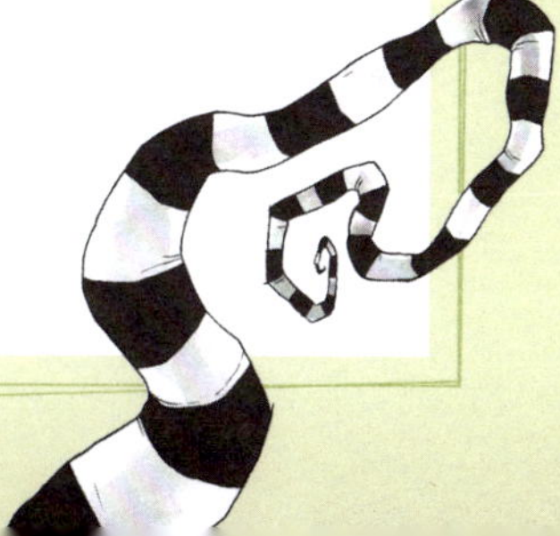

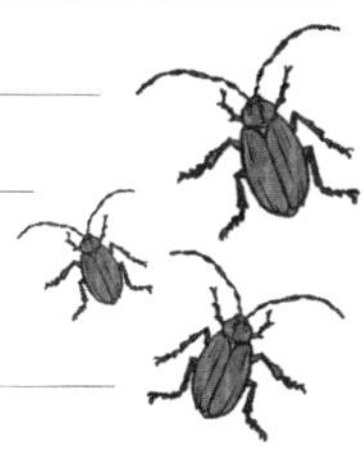

DATE __/__/__

TAROT READING

MOON PHASE

Who is the tarot spread for?

QUERY

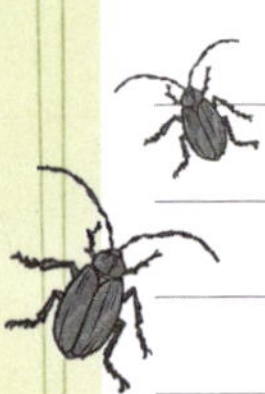

CARDS SELECTED

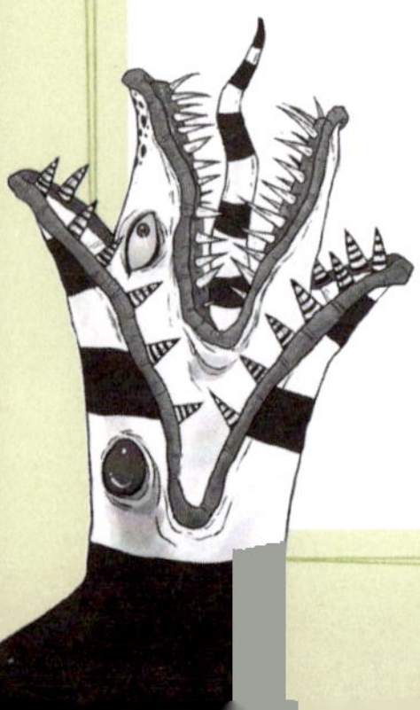

TAROT READING

INTERPRETATIONS

Thoughts and feelings:

DRAW YOUR SPREADS HERE

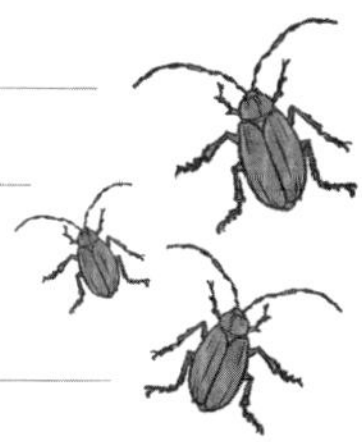

DATE __/__/__

TAROT READING

MOON PHASE

Who is the tarot spread for?

QUERY

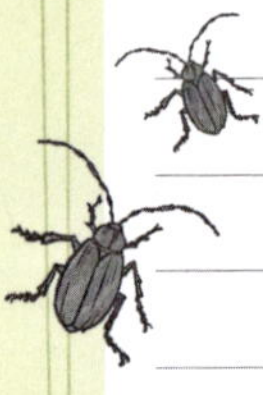

CARDS SELECTED

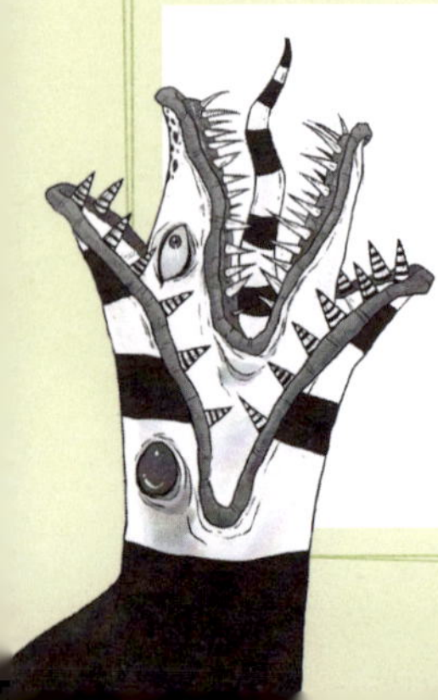

TAROT READING

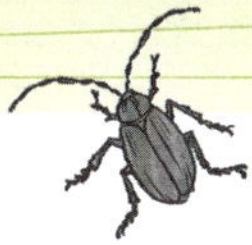

INTERPRETATIONS

Thoughts and feelings:

DRAW YOUR SPREADS HERE

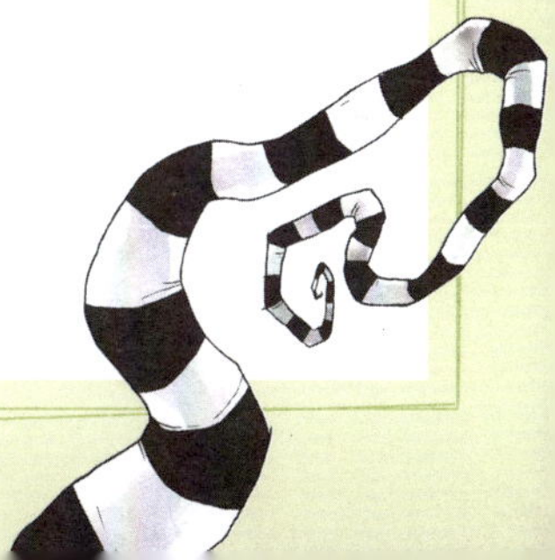

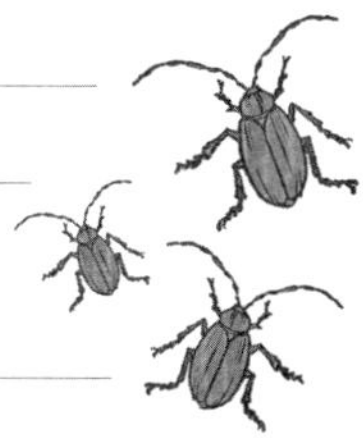

DATE __/__/__

TAROT READING

MOON PHASE

Who is the tarot spread for?

QUERY

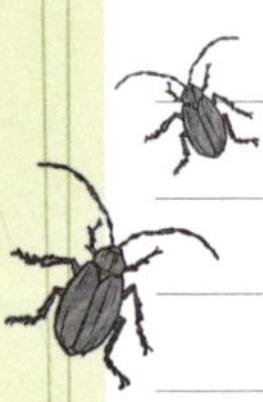

CARDS SELECTED

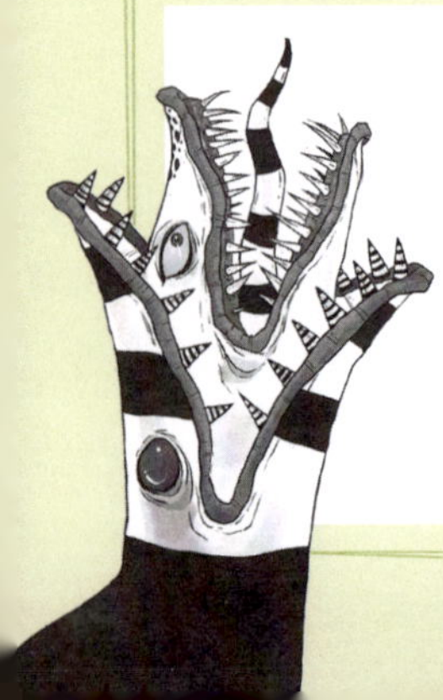

TAROT READING

INTERPRETATIONS

Thoughts and feelings:

DRAW YOUR SPREADS HERE

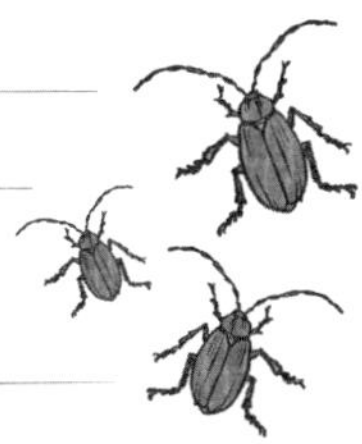

DATE __/__/__

TAROT READING

MOON PHASE

Who is the tarot spread for?

QUERY

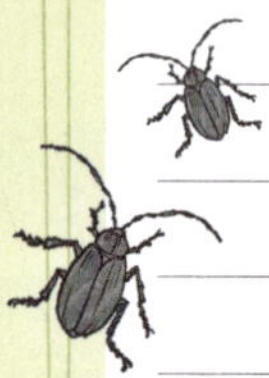

CARDS SELECTED

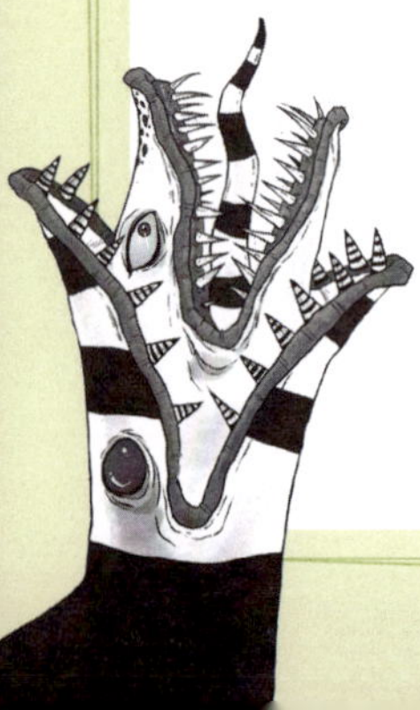

TAROT READING

INTERPRETATIONS

Thoughts and feelings:

DRAW YOUR SPREADS HERE

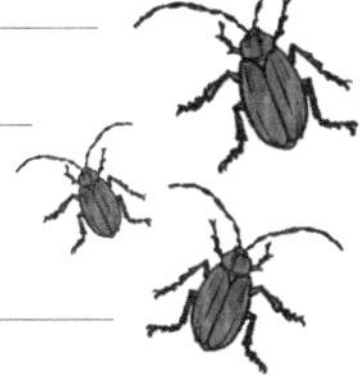

DATE __/__/__

TAROT READING

MOON PHASE

Who is the tarot spread for?

QUERY

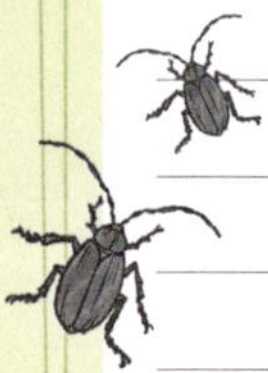

CARDS SELECTED

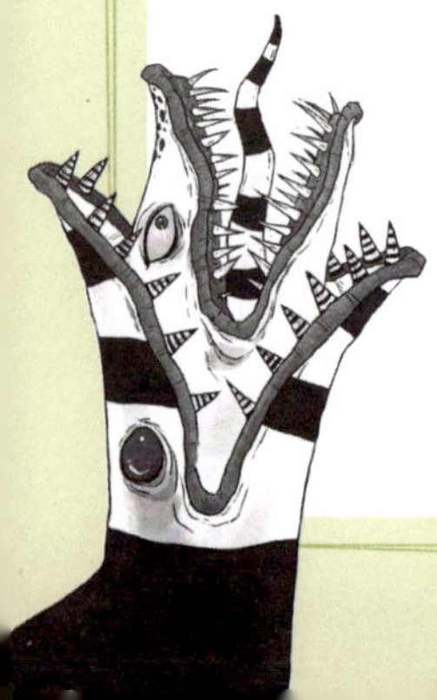

TAROT READING

INTERPRETATIONS

Thoughts and feelings:

DRAW YOUR SPREADS HERE

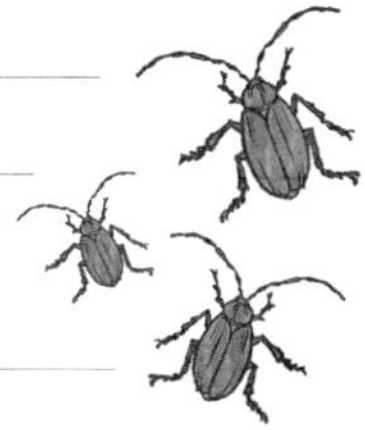

DATE __/__/__

TAROT READING

MOON PHASE

Who is the tarot spread for?

QUERY

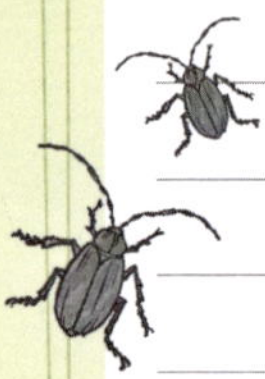

CARDS SELECTED

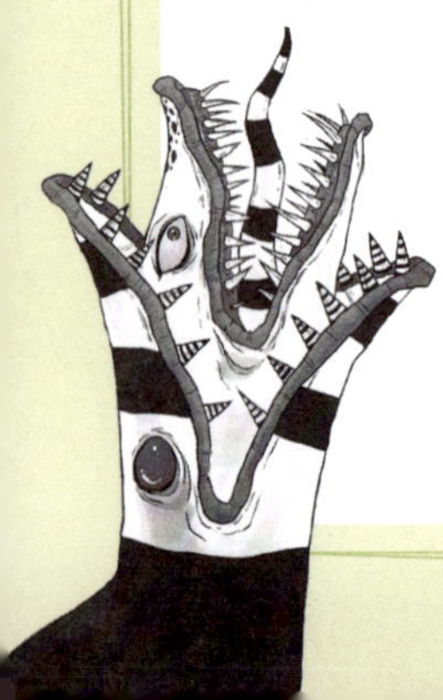

TAROT READING

INTERPRETATIONS

Thoughts and feelings:

DRAW YOUR SPREADS HERE

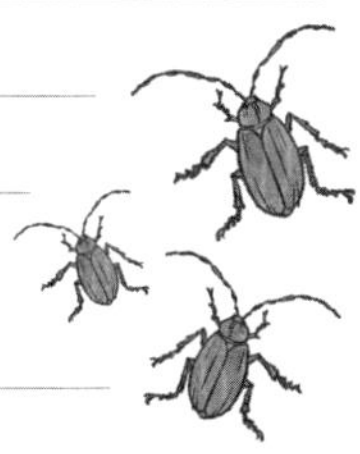

DATE __/__/__

TAROT READING

MOON PHASE

Who is the tarot spread for?

QUERY

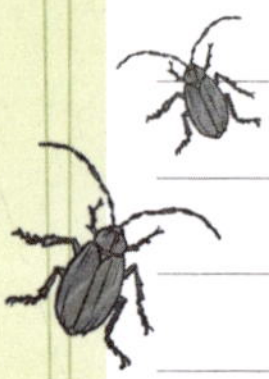

CARDS SELECTED

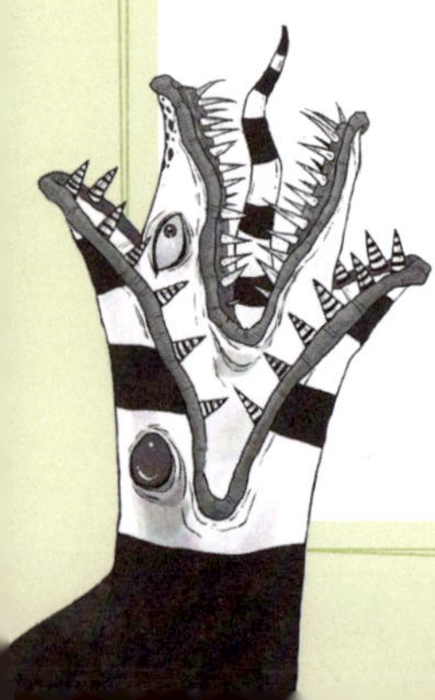

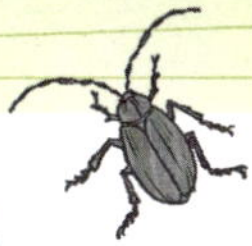

TAROT READING

INTERPRETATIONS

Thoughts and feelings:

DRAW YOUR SPREADS HERE

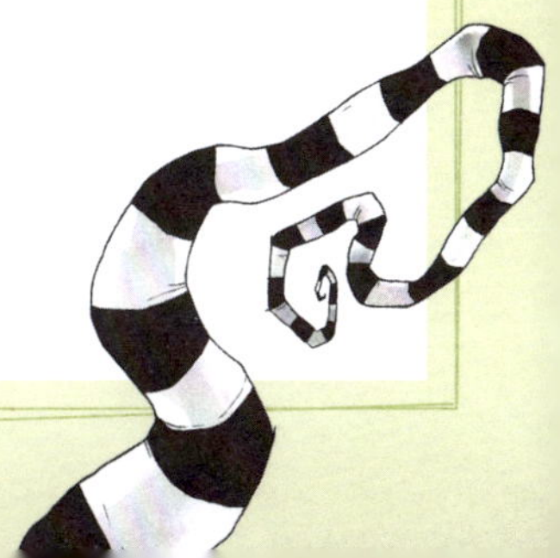

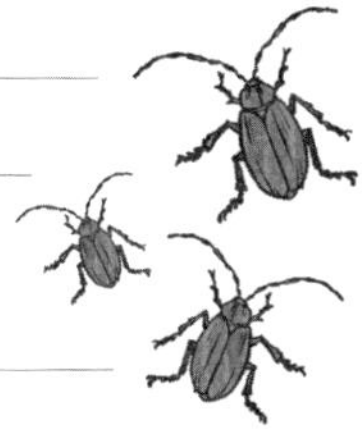

DATE __/__/__

TAROT READING

MOON PHASE

Who is the tarot spread for?

QUERY

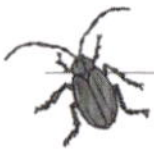

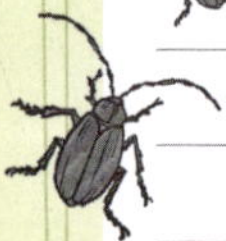

CARDS SELECTED

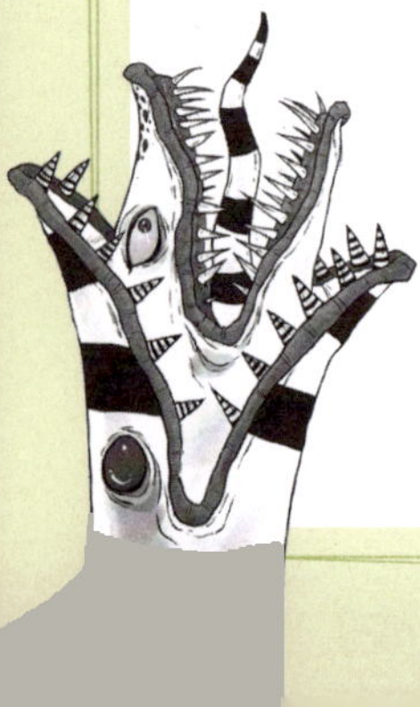

TAROT READING

INTERPRETATIONS

Thoughts and feelings:

DRAW YOUR SPREADS HERE

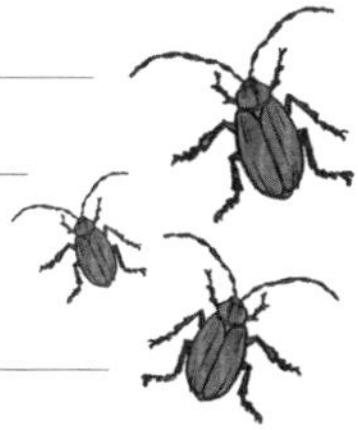

DATE __/__/__

TAROT READING

MOON PHASE

Who is the tarot spread for?

QUERY

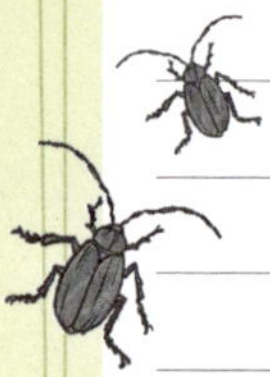

CARDS SELECTED

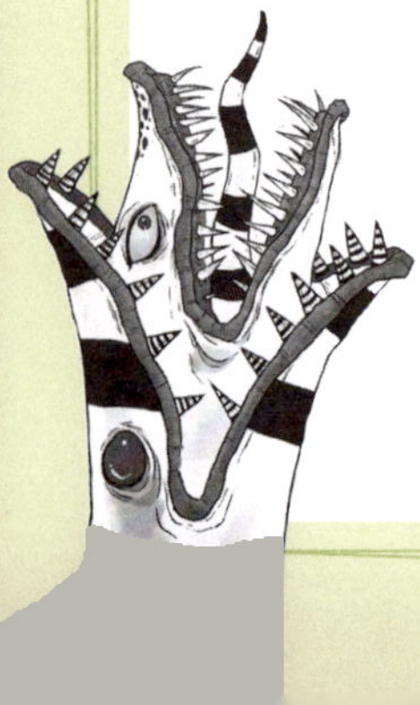

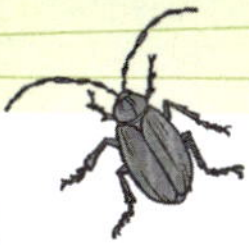

TAROT READING

INTERPRETATIONS

Thoughts and feelings:

DRAW YOUR SPREADS HERE

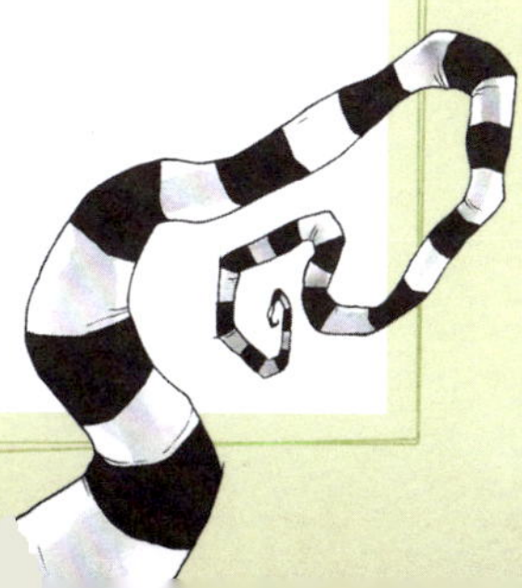

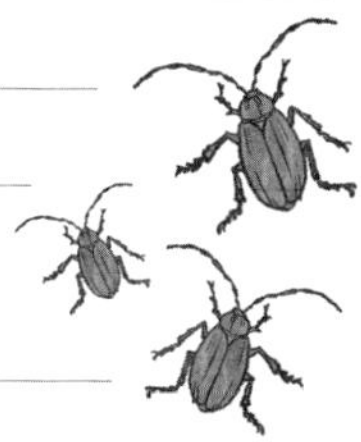

DATE __/__/__

TAROT READING

MOON PHASE

Who is the tarot spread for?

QUERY

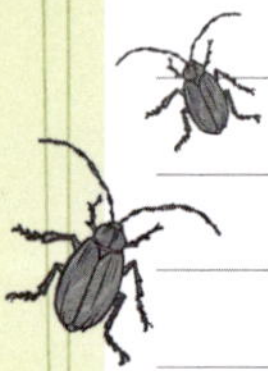

CARDS SELECTED

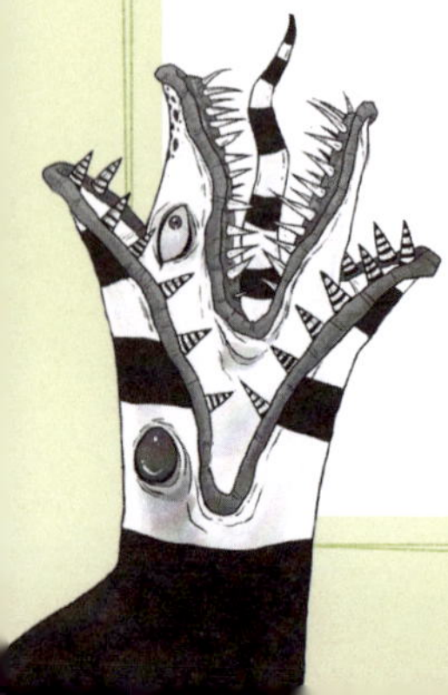

TAROT READING

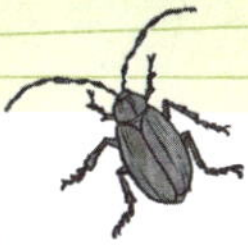

INTERPRETATIONS

Thoughts and feelings:

DRAW YOUR SPREADS HERE

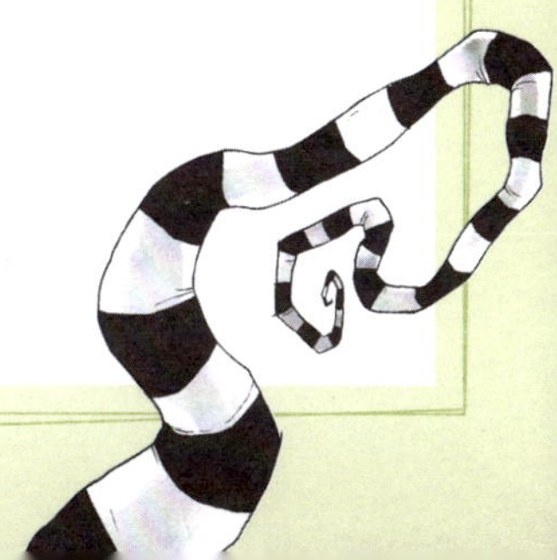

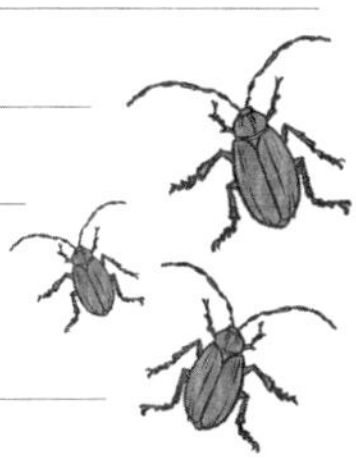

DATE __/__/__

TAROT READING

MOON PHASE

Who is the tarot spread for?

QUERY

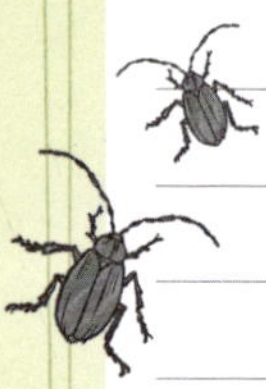

CARDS SELECTED

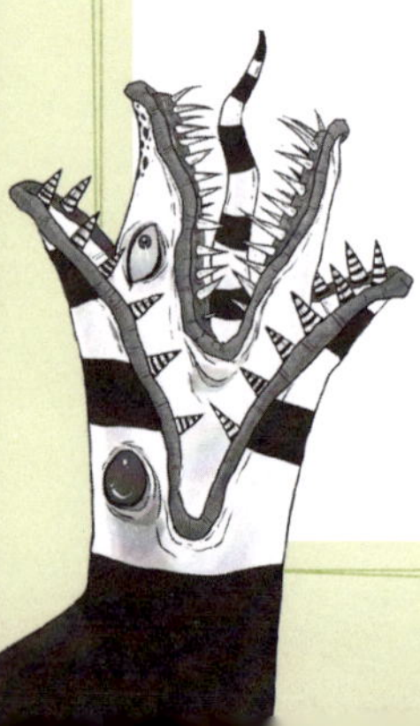

TAROT READING

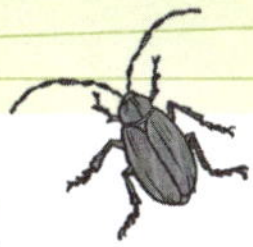

INTERPRETATIONS

Thoughts and feelings:

DRAW YOUR SPREADS HERE

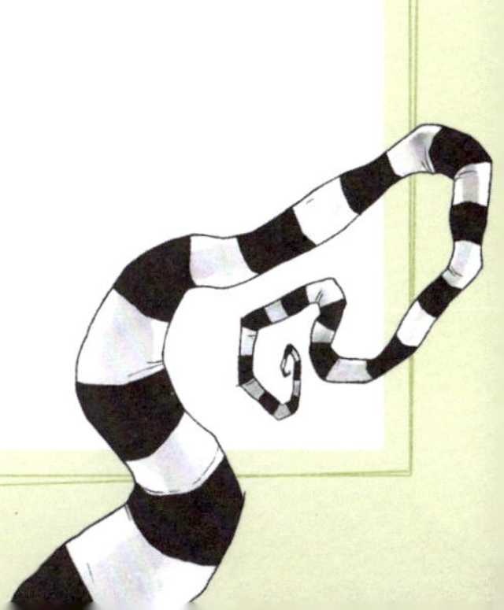

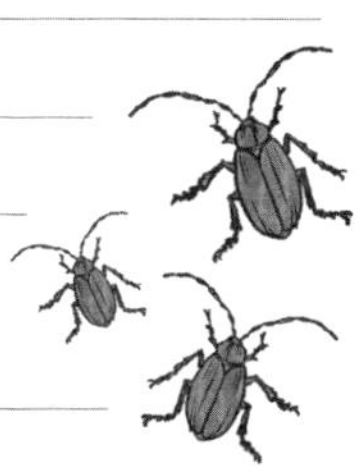

DATE __/__/__

TAROT READING

MOON PHASE

Who is the tarot spread for?

QUERY

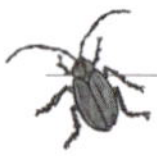

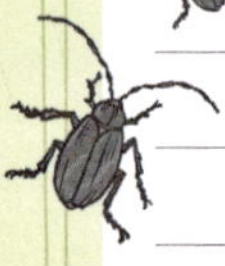

CARDS SELECTED

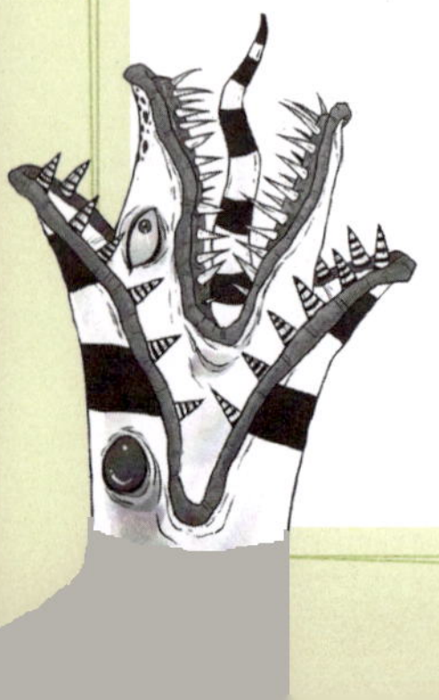

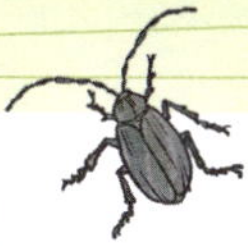

TAROT READING

INTERPRETATIONS

Thoughts and feelings:

DRAW YOUR SPREADS HERE

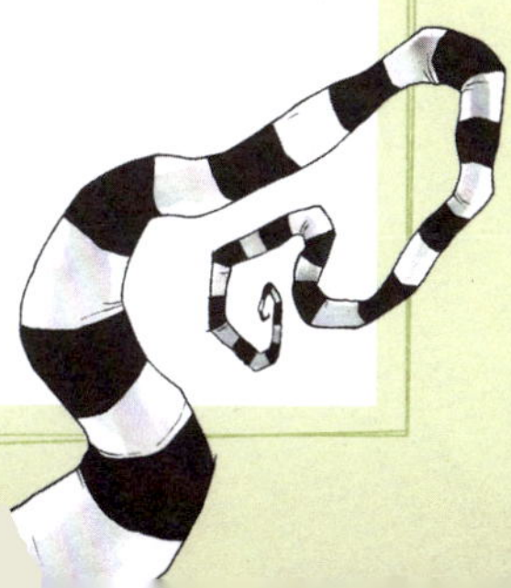

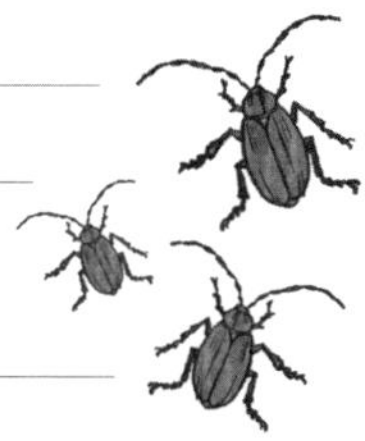

DATE __/__/__

TAROT READING

MOON PHASE

Who is the tarot spread for?

QUERY

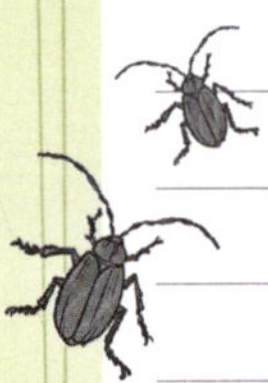

CARDS SELECTED

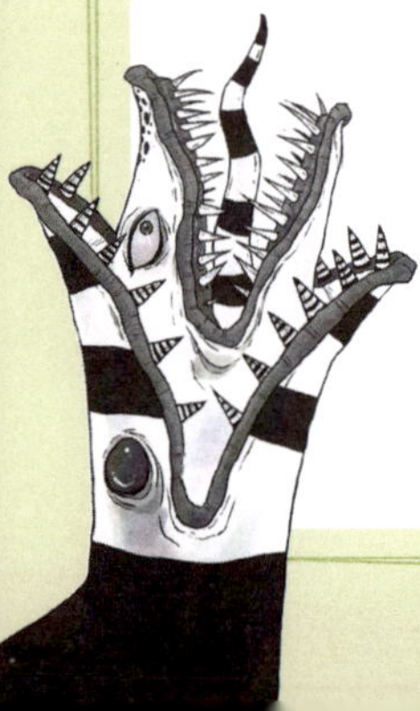

TAROT READING

INTERPRETATIONS

Thoughts and feelings:

DRAW YOUR SPREADS HERE

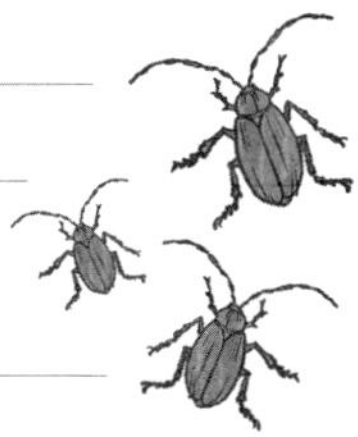

DATE __/__/__

TAROT READING

MOON PHASE

Who is the tarot spread for?

QUERY

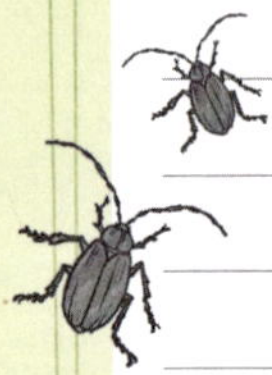

CARDS SELECTED

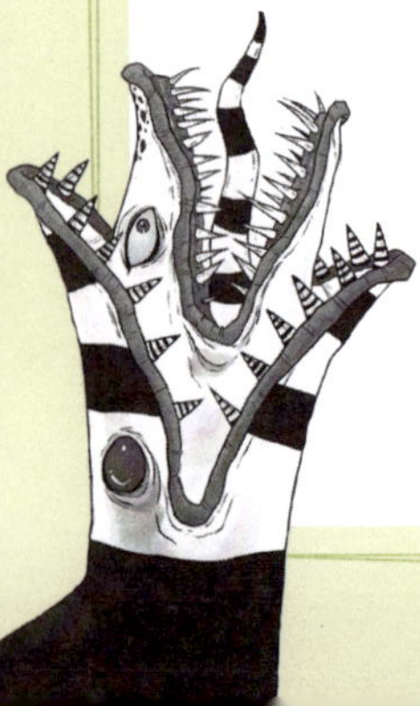

TAROT READING

INTERPRETATIONS

Thoughts and feelings:

DRAW YOUR SPREADS HERE

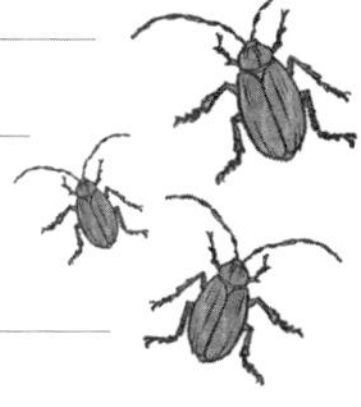

DATE __/__/__

TAROT READING

MOON PHASE

Who is the tarot spread for?

QUERY

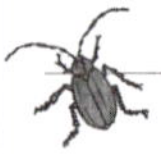

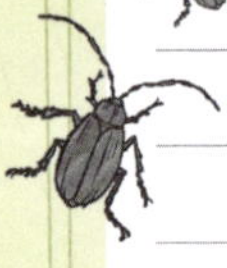

CARDS SELECTED

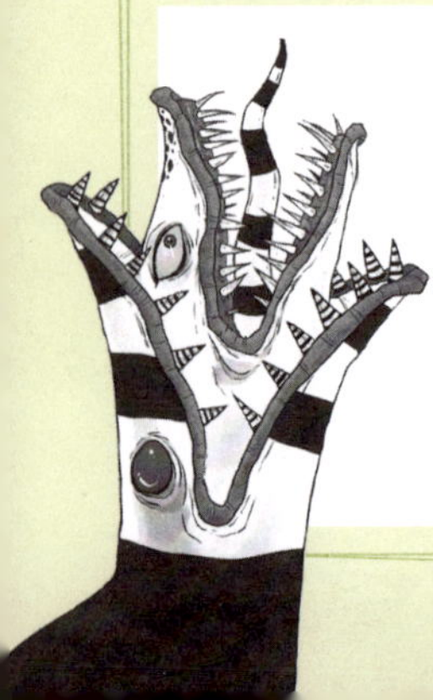

TAROT READING

INTERPRETATIONS

Thoughts and feelings:

DRAW YOUR SPREADS HERE

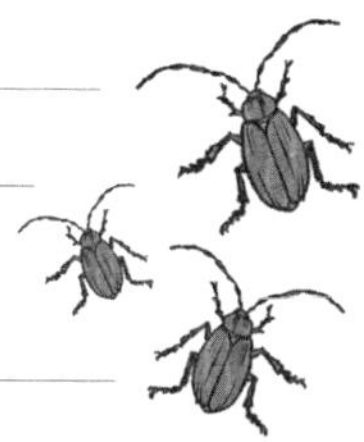

DATE __/__/__

TAROT READING

MOON PHASE

Who is the tarot spread for?

QUERY

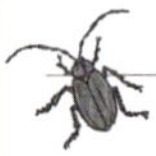

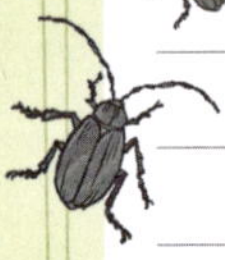

CARDS SELECTED

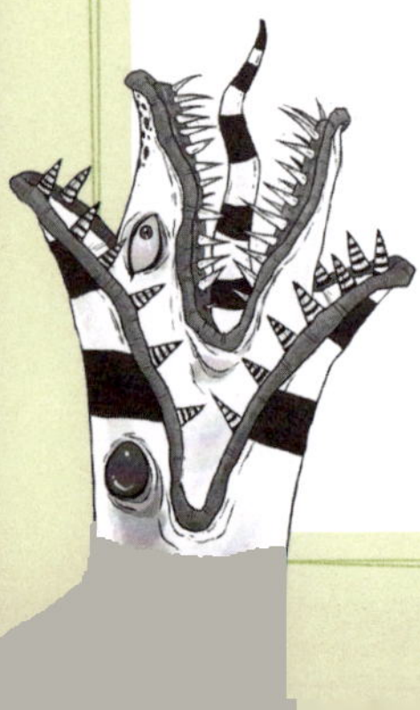

TAROT READING

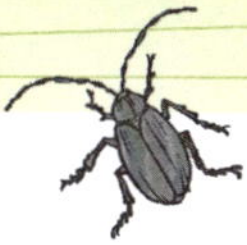

INTERPRETATIONS

Thoughts and feelings:

DRAW YOUR SPREADS HERE

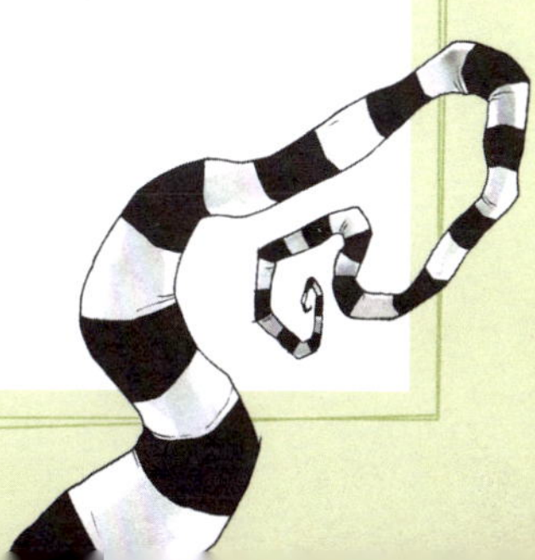

INSIGHT
EDITIONS
insighteditions.com

Manufactured in China

10 9 8 7 6 5 4 3 2 1